Table of C

PREAMBLE..5

PART 1: SOCIAL ALIENATION 9

1. The Good Ship Rainbow 10

2. Reporting Consistently on Racism..14

3. No one is Perfect..20

4. Identity Politics is our Default Drive 25

5. Victims can be Black or White, the Point is – they are Victims......30

6. Is "Implicit Bias" the new term for "Closed Racism"? 37

8. Out of Apartheid; into a de facto Two State Solution 45

9. From Hardened Attitudes to Balkanization 50

10. How Not to Impair the Dignity of Fellow Citizens 56

11. Forget Anger Management, we need Greed Therapy...........60

PART 2: POLITICAL PRECEDENTS..66

13. A Laager of Exclusion? 73

14. Pan-Africanism Going Forward..77

15. From Riding Hobby Horses to Riding the Zebra 81

16. South Africa's Crown of Thorns...86

17. The Pot Calling the Kettle White.......................................90

18. Don't call me "Babe X" 96

PART 3: UP CLOSE AND PERSONAL 142

25. Where does the African Renaissance end and Black Supremacy begin?...143

ORANIA AND AZANIA

ORANIA AND AZANIA

If Social Cohesion is not Right

Then only **Balkanization** is **Left**

By

C O Stephens

Orania and Azania

Publication © 2020 Mbokodo Publishers

Text © 2020 CO Stephens

ISBN-13: 978-1-990919-06-0 (Paperback)

ISBN-13: 978-1-990919-07-7 (PDF)

ISBN-13: 978-1-990919-08-4 (eBook)

Publisher: M.R. Mbokodo

Proofreading: CO Stephens

Cover Design: M.R. Mbokodo

Photo Credit: IEC, 2019 Elections

Published by

Typeset in 10/12 Adobe Garamond Pro by Mbokodo Publishers

Printed by Mbokodo Publishers 1 2 3 4 5 1 2

mbokodopublishers@gmail.com

PREAMBLE

THE names Orania and Azania are used more metaphorically than physically in this book. Nevertheless the right starting point is to define them.

Orania is a place. Symbolically, it lies half way between Capetown and Pretoria. It is unashamedly Afrikaner. The town exists to perpetuate Afrikaans culture and language. It is sort of a "reverse homeland", the opposite pole to the concept of a Rainbow Nation.

Self-reliance and the right to self-determination are high on its agenda. It seems anachronistic, but it is thriving. There is no crime, the residents don't have to even lock their doors. There are no potholes in the roads. People quite literally just mind their own business. Its economy is booming. It is not exactly a Boer republic or a Volkstaat, but it resonates with that kind of thinking.

The difference between Orania and the Palestinian Authority or the island to which the Rohingya are being sequestered off the coast of Myanmar is that residents are living in this Karoo town by choice. The <u>Los Angeles Times</u> called it "a bastion of intolerance". The <u>Mail & Guardian</u> called it a "media byword for racism and irredentism". (An irredentist is "one who advocates restoration to his country of all territory formerly belonging to it".)

When interviewed by the media in the run-up to the 2019 elections, Orania's leaders declared that their Vision was not about colour. If blacks or coloureds want to adopt Afrikaans as their language and assimilate into its culture with due respect, then they would be welcome (so they said). It sounds a bit theoretical, but that is the official line.

Azania is the erstwhile name for South Africa. Just as Rhodesia became Zimbabwe and Zambia, and Swaziland has become eSwatini, radical politicians have dreamed of re-naming South Africa. Pretoria has become Tshwane; Nelspruit has become Mbombela; and so on.

Azania seems to be a Greek word borrowed by Latin to name the south-eastern side of Africa. By comparison, the word "Africa" has its roots in the Egyptian language – "Afru-ika" meaning "motherland". However, Narius Moloto, the General Secretary of the PAC claims that the name *Azania* is derived from the term Azanj which is Arabic. All of the above could be true, as the Greeks could have learned it from Arabic and passed it on to the Romans.

As this was all before migrations of waBantu crossed from West Africa into eastern and southern Africa, the original Azanians could be either Nilotics or the Ba Boroa. In East Africa there are tall black people like the waTutsi and the Dinkas, as well as short people like the pygmies who also preceded Bantus in the Ituri forest. The first nations or aboriginal peoples of southern Africa were the Khoi and the San (or Khoisan) – now called the Ba Baroa. Both of these are difference races to one another and to the waBantu – they are not just distinct tribes.

The Economic Freedom Fighters or EFF are the latest political force to articulate the need to drop all names with colonial connotations. Just as Jan Smuts airport was re-named after Oliver Tambo, the EFF is pressing for Capetown's airport to be name after Winnie Madikizela-Mandela.

Floyd Shivambu says that the EFF would like to rename South Africa – "Azania".

Re-naming never ends. Upper Volta is now Burkina Faso. Persia is now Iran. Ceylon is now Sri Lanka. Burma is now Myanmar. And so on.

The real concern that is the focus of this book is when white supremacy is replaced by black supremacy. If you think it's odd that a white minority could rule South Africa, then what about affirmative action in favour of a majority? Eighty-one percent of South African citizens are black. Nine percent are coloured. Eight percent are white. Two percent are Indian. Yet affirmative action policies favour the non-whites. Why does a majority need affirmative action in its favour?

In this book, these two terms – Orania and Azania - are mostly metaphorical. They are symbolic of a trending that has many precedents in recent history:

- North Korea and South Korea
- Ireland and Northern Ireland
- West Pakistan and East Pakistan (EP is now Bangladesh)
- East Berlin and West Berlin
- East Germany and West Germany
- Eastern Europe and Western Europe
- Israel and Palestine
- China and Taiwan

The trending that seems all but inevitable, is that South Africa may split into a "Two State Solution". To capture this sense of direction, this book uses these two terms very loosely – Orania for the western portion of the African sub-continent (not just for the town) and Azania for the eastern portion (including enclaves like Lesotho and eSwatini).

The results of the 2019 election help to visualize this trending. They are placed here now for shock value, although they are only discussed in Part 2 of the book.

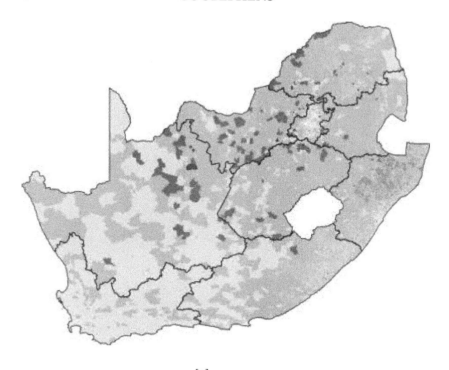

Image source: IEC, 2019 Elections[1]

A legend is not needed here – to indicate which party won where. All that one needs to do is to visualize the split that is emerging – Orania to the south and west and Azania to the east and north. The biggest tribe in Azania is the Zulus, who are very traditional and proudly African. So the recovery of their Inkatha Freedom Party in the 2019 elections lines up with the nearby presence of Lesotho and eSwatini in the "green zone".

This book is not written to cheer or champion this trending. If anything, it has been keyboarded as a wake-up call. The fact that this is happening is not good. But the fact is, it is happening.

PART 1: SOCIAL ALIENATION

1. The Good Ship Rainbow

IN 2016, two shocking stories rocked the good ship *Rainbow*. She is still afloat, but taking on water fast. They occurred in different seasons but within but a few kilometers of one another.

In July, in one of the country's highest and coldest town, Pierre Etienne de Necker was bludgeoned to death with bottles and pipes – by 12 men. This happened in Belfast Extension 2 on July 12th 2016.

One of the murderers crassly took a photo of the dying fellow with his cell-phone and sent it to his sister to brag of what he and 11 others had done. His sister posted it on Facebook. Someone who knew De Necker saw it, recognized him, and phoned his family to notify them. Almost a million adults-over-18 got to see that photo, all over the world.

It was a torpedo into the good ship *Rainbow* - on the port side. It was a hate-murder. Twelve people attacking one seems like cowardice to me, not something to brag about. If 11 of them had formed a ring and put up one among them to fight De Necker, inside the ring, that might seem more like a level playing field. And less like a lynching.

They say he had stolen a vehicle. They say that vigilantes are more effective than the police. They say that the police delayed in responding and that the ambulance delayed in rushing him to the hospital. It starts to sound positively structural.

Only a month later, and not far away, two young whites on a farm near Middelburg forced a black man into a coffin. Two against one – on their turf. This happened on August 27th 2016 but was not reported by the victim until mid-November.

One of the two perpetrators had a gun, so they tied him up and forced him into a coffin. Near an open grave. He was afraid that they would bury him alive. He was so scared that he didn't report it. Strangely, the story was leaked by the perpetrators.

It first appeared on YouTube on November 7th. In the 20-second video, a man speaking in Afrikaans threatens to burn him alive while they throw petrol on him. The good ship *Rainbow* was torpedoed again – this time on the starboard side.

They say he was trespassing. He says that he was following a footpath. Victor Mlotshwa didn't think the police would believe him. Until the video emerged on YouTube. Using phones to brag about the scene of a crime has reached crisis proportions.

Why do we treat one another this way?

And why do we hear mainly about what whites-do-to-blacks in the national news? I suppose because of the country's hideous history, which was totally one-sided. The media may be trying to redress that? That was certainly the way it was, but now there are about 6 million whites living among 49 million blacks. Totalling 55 million. Who is outnumbered? Who feels the most stress?

At what stage will the media offer "equal time" to both such incidents?

It occurred to me that when Hitler came to power in 1933, the Nazis wasted no time in putting the heat on the Jews. Within months, there were government-led initiatives like book-bonfires and boycotts of Jewish shops. They only burned books written by Jews. Like Sigmund Freud and Albert Einstein. And they did this at midnight - to conjure up the ancient spirits of pre-Christian Germanic gods... after marching through the streets – only after dark – bearing torches on the way to light the bonfires. This was intentionally pagan, to intimidate the

Church as well. Plus, it is always sinister when a majority harasses a minority – but in South Africa, with its deeply embedded ethos of affirmative action, this is rarely mentioned and then denied when someone mentions it.

The ratio of whites and blacks is the same in the USA and South Africa – only there, the 10 percent is African-American and here it is white. One key difference is that the 10 percent here is mostly rich, whereas the 10 percent in the USA emerged from Slavery and thus started on the back foot in economic terms. Although they are rich in other ways. They have begun to accumulate capital now, and education, and power. All the way to the White House.

Even Barrack Obama was vocal about anti-black sentiments that linger. But remember that is government protecting the minority. Whereas the death camps of the Holocaust, brought to you by the Nazis, was a case of the majority - in government - exterminating a targeted minority. Hate crimes. Ethnic cleansing.

At the time of the Treason Trials, Nelson Mandela stated bravely and wisely:

"During my lifetime I have dedicated myself to this struggle of the African people. I have fought against white domination, and I have fought against black domination. I have cherished the ideal of a democratic and free society in which all persons will live together in harmony and with equal opportunities. It is an ideal which I hope to live for. But, my lord, if needs be, it is an ideal for which I am prepared to die."

We have to find one another before the good ship *Rainbow* sinks. We should see this in balanced perspective. There are perpetrators and victims - on both sides. They all equally deserve action by law enforcement that will constitute a deterrent. Vigilantes and gangsters do not solve the problem, they compound it. Slow response from police and incident management hurts victims black and white.

2. Reporting Consistently on Racism

In mid-October 2016 there was a conference in Joburg convened by the Institute for the Advancement of Journalism called *Reporting Race*. You can't read anything into the fact that it was attended by more blacks than whites – that is just demographically accurate. The awareness that I came away with from attending this event made me watch closely in my province of Mpumalanga as such stories emerged...

In retrospect, thinking of the stories of Victor Mlotshwa and Etienne de Necker, I have a sense that while both these stories were reported on, if one counted the "column-inches" involved, I think that the story of the black victim got much more coverage? Since then, I have been trying to keep a monitoring eye on whether both sides are reported on equitably.

In May 2017, in Mbombela, there was a huge row over the way four white golfers, older men, assaulted one 19-year black golfer on the course. They beat him up and made it clear that he was unwelcome, although he was a professional golfer. Again there was something of a delayed response to this incident, which happened in October 2016. But the local media did report on this story, including coverage of the protests and demonstrations that it provoked. The political back-lash of the incident put pressure on Mbombela Local Municipality to cancel its lease to the Nelspruit Golf Club (NGC).

In the meanwhile there was an ugly event in a Spur restaurant. Part of this altercation (not all) was also captured on a cell-phone and went viral. It was a verbal exchange between two parents, a white man and a black woman. It raised questions about double-standards.

Most restaurants have mainly black staff, and mainly white managers, although these stereotypes are fading. This incident cost Spur big-time, because whites responded with a boycott that caused some of its franchises a huge loss of income. Mainly in settings where white farmers are its main customers.

Georgina Guedes wrote this in an opinion piece on eNCA: *"To the eyewitness apologist and all the other people who have been saying that Lebogang Mabuya was "unladylike" and that she "shouldn't have sworn at him" or that they are "both to blame" for what happened or that "she was asking for it", are you watching the same version of events that I am?"*

In fact, this altercation was a proxy-war that started in the playground between their two children. They say that it was not racism; it was more about gender-and-child-abuse. The focus of the boycott was that anti-white racism is rarely given "equal time". And/or that the same can be said about "male-bashing" by feminists. Men usually pay the bill at the end of a meal at Spur and they registered their discontent with the way its staff and managers handled this confrontation, by boycotting Spur. It put men and whites in a generally bad light, which is not the whole story.

#StopRacism

At trade union Solidarity's #StopRacism conference later in 2017, best-selling author, historian and former Oxford don RW Johnson was one of the keynote speakers. In his view, the ruling alliance's increasingly vocal racist rhetoric is a decoy – to distract attention away from its monumental failings. This has the effect of enriching and reinforcing the politically connected.

Johnson has been around long enough to have observed the way *swart gevaar* was used as a strategy of racial mobilization. As he put it: *"Now, it's happening against whites and I would say that public racism has always been one-sided. I don't think it's ever been an equal thing and I don't think it ever can be. When I was a kid; if a black man raped my white woman, he was hanged. If it was the other way around and a white man raped a black woman, he'd get a fine or a short sentence. It was, quite obviously, not an equal law and that was just commonplace."*

He explained that this has now turned around. He does not feel that anti-white racism is given "equal time". The same is true in terms of Gender. There is such a strong Feminist lobby embedded in public institutions now that men find it hard to get a fair shake.

If RW Johnson is right, this imbalance in reporting could be intentional – to distract attention away from the monumental failings of a government that is preoccupied with white domination and that practices black domination.

Crimes are crimes are crimes – no matter what the skin colour of the perpetrators. God help us to replace this preoccupation with race long enough to make a real distinction between the good guys and the bad guys. There are good citizens and criminals on both sides of the colour bar, after all.

The notion of "white monopoly capital" has been debated hotly since it was revived by Bell-Pottinger in a cynical attempt to pour oil onto this fire. Well what about "black ballot capital" in a country where blacks out-number whites ten-to-one? There are now more Coloured/Indians (non-whites and non-blacks) than there are whites as well. Given these proportions, the rare reporting on racism-that-targets-whites does not bode well for transparency and non-racialism.

The way that whites have treated blacks will certainly be an election issue in the push for "land expropriation without compensation". There was another snapshot of this in the EFF's motion to remove a Mayor – "because he is white". His party disagreed with the EFF's policy platform, but the language of EFF's rationale was ugly. The way the majority treats minorities is always an issue in constitutional democracies. Just as black voices have objected to the EFF's anti-white rhetoric in Nelson Mandela Bay, the recovery of – or rejection of – the "Rainbow Nation" will be a hot issue in future elections. Perhaps in the guise of a debate over affirmative action?

Case Study

One Mpumalanga case that is currently under investigation involves both aspects – race and gender. It blends three criminal activities in a cunning way. First, the deployment of a woman for Lobola in a "fake marriage". These scams have been reported on widely in the media, and are one of the reasons that the Zulu king has terminated Lobola for his tribe. But they usually involve black men from other African countries where Customary Marriages are also the norm, that are lonely and want a local bride. So there is an element of xenophobia in the mix.

Second, there can be a racial spin on this - when the lonely man is a white foreigner looking for a companion. One of the realities of negotiating Lobola locally, especially when you don't speak the vernacular, is that you have to depend a lot on trust and goodwill. Essentially you are outnumbered and thus isolated. There are inherent risks.

Third, there is the near and present danger of HIV, with South Africa's high prevalence. Especially among women, and all the more so among lawless women. And there IS such a thing as "harmful HIV transmission" (a k a "HIV-endangerment") so this scourge can even be the very weapon used to take you out. (So that the woman and her accomplices can obtain your wealth.) This scenario is not so far-fetched in a country where stories of one spouse killing the other are frequently in the news. Ask Fish Mahlalela!

The deep background to this is the case of Lovers Phiri. He was employed as a counselor in an AIDS clinic. So he knew the ground-rules. Yet he preyed upon a young woman who had just broken up with her husband, and was desperately trying to support her child. When they had sex, he didn't use a condom. She got the virus, and thus reported him. He was convicted in Piet Retief, Mpumalanga – of attempted murder.

While languishing in jail, he appealed his conviction and 6-year prison term, saying that transmission had occurred in the context of a "love relationship". The High Court's decision upheld his conviction and sentencing, saying that (in paragraph 15 of the judgment): *"The argument that because there was a love relationship between the parties should serve as a mitigating factor, is a startling proposition. We do not perceive how this could possibly serve as a mitigating factor. That very fact could easily serve as an aggravating one, as lovers are expected to protect one another."*

Now imagine an older white male trying to argue that his black *makoti* behaved recklessly – putting him in harm's way. As no one can negotiate their own Lobola, she was a deployee of a team. It turns out that Lobola had previously been collected from another man for the same lady! (Although in Tsonga culture, Lobola is never paid more than once for the same woman.) There were other discrepancies too, that emerged ex-post – but do you think that given the combined race and gender aspects, this case will ever be reported on by the media? Or investigated by the police? Or prosecuted by the NPA? Dream on!

When the Proceedings of the World Conference against Racism, Racial Discrimination, Xenophobia and Related Intolerance emerged in 2001, this clause was included in the Preamble - reminiscent of the Rwanda genocide which was a recent memory at that time: *"Alarmed by the emergence and continued occurrence of racism, racial discrimination, xenophobia and related intolerance in their more subtle and contemporary forms and manifestations, as well as by other ideologies and practices based on racial or ethnic discrimination or superiority."*

Reporting on racism is always going to be hard to put on an even keel. Because by its very nature, someone is implicitly trying to put someone else down. The media can never be impartial, but it must try to be consistent. Starting with reporting both sides of the story.

3. No one is Perfect

Being the director of a leadership centre, I watch leaders very closely. It is certainly rare to find one who is consistently above reproach.

My sense of fair play has made it hard for me to swallow the way the Mayor of Capetown was sidelined before she quit and started her new party called GOOD. My generally positive views of the DA's young leader at the time was shaken by my habitual inclination to side with the underdog. (No offence meant by that term to the then-Mayor, who has now been coopted as a Minister in the Cabinet.) The only good thing one could see in it, is that the DA had the courage to tackle an incumbent leader, not just to sweep the smallanyana skeletons under the carpet or into the closet.

I was so disgusted by Zuma's last Cabinet shuffle (in 2017) that I wrote a short article called *"March 31st will go down in history as Banana Republic Day"*. The way that then-Finance Minister Gordhan and others were treated was very, very shabby. It was the last straw for many citizens (read: voters), triggering what can only be called a "citizen revolt".

Now that president has been replaced... and Nene, Gordhan, and Hanekom all came back. There was something delicious about this irony.

The deadwood that was cleared away by Ramaphosa in his first Cabinet shuffle - like Mahlobo, van Rooyen, and Brown – was no surprise. If anything, we were surprised that Dlamini, Gigaba, Mokonyane and Muthambi were not dispatched as well, for their respective bungling and/or linkages to State Capture.

No tears were shed over Shaun the sheep Abraham's departure either, when the High Court's decision was validated by the Constitutional Court. All of these follow a consistent logic; they were rational steps all going in the right direction.

But I personally have a bone to pick with the EFF over its decision to abandon the coalition in Nelson Mandela Bay, sacking Mayor Trollip. This seemed vindictive.

In their book The Fall of the ANC, Mashele and Qobo call the breed of leaders that came to the fore after Polokwane: "vindictive triumphalists". The ANC leadership style that prevailed after Polokwane was brazen and unprincipled. The other camp within the ANC was dubbed by these two authors too: "soul-battered mourners". We saw some of these emerge like Makhosi Khoza, the Stalwarts, Ahmed Kathrada, and so forth.

I have admired the EFF's intolerance of corruption and ANC vindictiveness. Less than a year after Malema was turfed out of the ANC (a soul-battered mourner if there ever was one), he formed a new party and won 25 seats in a parliament of 400 seats. That was amazing. (What is more amazing is that even following the VBS scandal, the EFF increased its contingent to 44 seats in the 2019 elections!)

The scuffles on the floor of Parliament and the *#PayBackTheMoney* campaign actually stole the DA's thunder and made the EFF look at times like the official opposition party. This could be why this neophyte (pun intended) became the official opposition party in three provinces after the 2019 elections.

The EFF's response to the shock results of the Municipal elections in 2016 was to support the Coalitions in the Metros, while staying at arm's length. This allowed the DA time and space to really clean house and to expose the extent of the looting and plundering that had been going on. Triumphalism had reigned and the need for a massive clean-up was verified.

So it was alarming to me to suddenly see Malema throw the toys out of his crib and turn "vindictive triumphalist" himself – on Mayor Trollip.

Worse yet is the fact that there were three such municipal Coalitions – with two black Mayors and one white. One can only wonder why the EFF singled out the white Mayor - one who *exceptionally* was fluent in isiXhosa. He was symbolic. This made his removal look like it was anti-white.

If the DA's strong suite has been speaking up for non-racialism, then the EFF's strong suite has been speaking up for land redistribution. I was even pleased to see a committee set up in parliament to study how to amend the Constitution, if that is required to go forward with land reform. That was never going to be an easy prospect, and the EFF should never assume that just because a committee was set up, that the end-game will suit them. Sometimes setting up a committee is a good way to confuse matters! (It is said that a camel was the outcome of a committee's task to design a horse.) One must remember that the ANC's terminology of "unity" is code-language for "gridlock". There are at least two ANCs at this stage, if not more. Not everyone inside the ANC agrees that expropriation of land without compensation is the best way forward. EFF should not count its chickens before they hatch. What would happen if this is put to a secret vote?

Above all, I was disturbed by the racial overtones of the lunge at Mayor Trollip. Did the EFF really ever think that the DA might support its expropriation without compensation platform? Get serious! You cannot change the leopard's spots. The ANC maybe? But not the DA!

The DA comes from a "liberal" upbringing and the link of liberal democracy to property rights is systemic. It will not abandon its primordial roots, which has caused it to take a turn for the worst.

What does it say about the EFF and the very real prospect of NO PARTY winning a majority in future elections? The trending is clear – both the big parties are shrinking and the size and number of smaller parties is growing. Who will want to form a coalition with turn-coats?

And seriously after the honeymoon period of "Ramaphoria", even as his clean-up operation picks up speed, do you think that voters are going to forgive and forget? It seems rather that voters are withdrawing their consent. Ten million of the 37 million in the Electorate didn't even register. And of the 27 million who did register, only 18 million cast their vote. While 19 million stayed away. What was there to celebrate in that scenario?

I think that this incident really exposed the true colours of the EFF. Bold black voices spoke out in Nelson Mandela Bay asking why the EFF would sell out its Coalition partners? Only to bring back those looters and plunderers again before the State Capture investigation is concluded?

Then came the VBS scandal, which put the EFF's Shivambu on the back foot. For a while there, he took it on the cheek just like the Guptas and Gavin Watson. For the next election campaign, EFF chairperson Dali Mpofu had to step into the limelight. This was diversionary tactics.

I think that the EFF turning on its partner in Nelson Mandela Bay was either a serious miscalculation, or a glimpse of that recessive ANC gene that dwells in the DNA of the EFF. It is identity politics. Malema is the one who once said that he would kill for Zuma. At the time, few dared to speak out against the vindictive triumphalists. But Desmond Tutu rebuked Malema, publicly, and also Zuma for not having corrected the young man right on the podium at the time, as an African elder should have done. That night, the head of a statue of Desmond Tutu in Port Elizabeth was cut off! In the morning, it was laying on the lawn at the foot of the statue. This was in 2008, a full seven years before the *#RhodesMustFall* campaign.

First it was *#TutuMustFall*. Now it is *#TrollipMustFall*. Shame on you, EFF, for being so vindictive.

4. Identity Politics is our Default Drive

We have to be intentional about it. Or it will become our nemesis. We have to tune in on the frequency of policy debate, and tune out of identity politics. In other words, we have to play the ball, not the man. Or we will find ourselves sinking into the incivility that is dogging American electioneering. We are polarizing fast, driven by this trending.

At the height of the "Troubles" in Ireland, a joke was going around. An Ulsterman was walking home one dark night after having a few drinks at the pub. Out of the shadows came a thug in a trenchcoat with his collar turned up, who stopped him in his tracks, pointing a gun at him. "Are you Protestant or Catholic?" the man asked. Eish, he thought to himself... if I say I'm Protestant, he will shoot me and the Catholics will claim it. But if I say I'm Catholic, he'll shoot me anyway, and the Protestants will claim it. He suddenly had an idea... "I'm Jewish!" he replied to the man pointing a gun at him. To which the man replied in his broad Irish accent: "Oi, I am the luckiest Arab in all of Ireland!"

Identity politics. At least in Ireland they had to ask you the question - if you were Protestant or Catholic. In South Africa, the different identities are visible to the naked eye.

The USA went through a rough patch after the election of Donald Trump. The rancor was not unprecedented. We had glimpsed it before. In 1998, for example, when then-President Bill Clinton was impeached by the self-righteous Republicans over his affair with a White House intern. That moment in an otherwise well-run presidency generated more heat than light – Clinton was not removed from office, just humiliated.

Going back further, to the late 1960s and early 1970s, when Richard Nixon was elected. The identity politics reached dangerous proportions as the civil rights movement and the anti-war lobby were synergizing. Draft-dodging and the emergence of the Black Panthers made it look and sound like some Americans were more loyal than others. Political assassinations rocked the prosperity of the post-war boom.

Back further in the 1930s, America had high unemployment rates like South Africa has today. In fact, the unemployment rate peaked at 13 percent in 1933 – the worst year of the "dirty thirties". South Africa's is already twice that! This caused so much discontent that government intervened in the economy as never before. Ramaphosa's "New Dawn" sounds very much like FDR's "New Deal" – in case you missed it!

But the Civil War 150 years ago was when identity politics boiled over. The South was essentially a plantation economy – rural, agrarian and based on an identity-aristocracy, the white slave owners. The harsh rhetoric of the Anti-Slavery Movement caused moderate politicians at first to adopt "containment" as a policy – to keep slavery only in the south, and not allow it to spread into the west. But the southern gentlemen took that policy personally, and soon started to secede. The new president Abraham Lincoln saw that as treason.

An interesting aside is that the great Confederate general Robert E Lee was personally against slavery and owned no slaves. But he took exception to a State being obliged by the federal government to eradicate Slavery. To him, each state was sovereign and should outlaw Slavery on its own. So by winning the war, Abraham Lincoln not only freed the slaves, but also sealed a "Union" which was far more centralized than the south's notion of a "Confederacy".

This all sounds a bit like Brexit – which was opposed by so many both in the British Isles and the European Union. To some people, secession is treason. This resonates with the way some people feel about expropriating land without compensation. Does government have the right to confiscate private property in a constitutional democracy? For over a century the die-hards championing private property have been the liberal democrats. In South Africa's politics, that means the DA. The ANC believes in more of a planned economy. It is even talking of nationalizing the Reserve Bank at this point. Of course the smaller parties like the EFF, over on the Left, take "Socialism" far more seriously than "individualism".

These days, there are identity issues that backstop the policy questions. Gender rights, ethnicity, and sexual orientation are examples of identities with strong lobbies.

What about the Ba Baroa? They are now objecting to being called "coloured" which was a label that left them nowhere – caught in no-man's land between black and white. And it misconstrued them for true *mulatos*. But they are now mobilizing and making a lot of noise in their own right. One chief has recently declared that he is the supreme ruler of Western Cape province.

And the Zulus are not happy about their land trust being expropriated so that the people inhabiting it can receive the same kind of land title, like other citizens do elsewhere. One school of thought – championed by the Leftist EFF - promotes a one-size-fits-all policy on land title, but identity politics is kicking in to take exception. This is what is meant by "identity politics is our default drive". Another way of saying it is that sooner or later, South Africans will always play the race card. Recently, President Ramaphosa signed a bill into law that enshrines the rights of traditional leaders. It is hard to reconcile aboriginal rights with other human rights – for example, gender.

In the USA, this trending was happening at a time when the economy is booming, before it crached into the Covid-19 pandemic. Whereas in South Africa, the economy has been shedding jobs for 25 years and inequality is getting worse not better.

The EFF did us a huge favour to get Land Reform onto the front burner. But to its surprise, it has found that most parties agree that this is an imperative, in one form or another. Not everyone agrees on HOW, but no one denies that it is a high priority. Maybe not as high as Job Creation? Or as the Covid-19 disaster? That depends on whether you see the ultimate Solution (the new "normal") as agrarian and rural. Or is it industrial and urban? The trending – all across Africa - is urbanization. The fact is that most black citizens of South Africa are township dwellers, not rural folk. Not any more.

When Abraham Lincoln started to conscript blacks into his Union army, Emancipation became a foregone conclusion. Soon the dream emerged of "forty acres and a mule" – the payback that soldiers would get after winning the war. Many did, but the roll-out was mixed. To summarize, there was a brief "back-to-the-land movement" after the Civil War, but after only a few decades, most blacks opted to urbanize (read: migrate to the North and West) and agriculture in America today is largely a white sector. Furthermore, it is largely a mechanized sector where food is produced by "factory-farms". Labour-intensive technology was left behind a long time ago. So one has to wonder whether re-distributing land is really a solution for unemployment?

The problem with EFF is that it has used identity politics to get Land Reform on the front burner. This approach is disingenuous. It makes it look like it was just a good bet to get re-elected. Politicians think only of the next election. Statesmen think of the next generation. We must get past the identity politics and think about the issues that affect all citizens. What about Food Security? What is the knock-on effect that land expropriation will have on the banking sector? Are there not strategies that will bring blacks and whites together in farming, instead of polarizing citizens even more than ever? Identity politics can get dangerous.

We need to stop thinking about who is black and who is white, and start thinking hard how red and blue can work together in effective Coalitions. For there is no doubt that the big parties are shrinking, and that smaller parties are growing – in size and in number.

5. Victims can be Black or White, the Point is – they are Victims

Criminalizing hate *crimes* is an important step in the right direction. The Equality Act helped a bit - with hate *speech*. But the new *Prevention and Combating of Hate Crimes and Hate Speech Bill* envisions a day when we will not only hear-no-evil, but see-no-evil either.

The draft law covers a wide scope: "race, gender, sex, which includes intersex, ethnic or social origin, color, sexual orientation, religion, belief, culture, language, birth, disability, HIV status, nationality, gender identity, albinism, and occupation or trade."

First, three comments about this long list. In South Africa it starts with race. In other countries it might start with gender, which has been on the "front burner" since the campaign of the Suffragettes got going a century ago, in the wake of the Abolition movement. But here in South Africa, what comes to mind first when you hear the term "hate crime" is racism, and the recent conviction and sentencing of those two white men for forcing a black man into a coffin is evidence of why it is high time that such acts be criminalized. Whether they are random or structural, they must be deplored. By the way, they were convicted and sentenced harshly. As it should be.

Second, one wonders why the terms "occupation" or "trade" was included in the list? Was it to protect some specific vocations like prostitution that are illegal, but mistakenly lumped with rights issues? There is no "P" in "LGBTI" but unlike other criminal occupations, there always seems to be some "space for grace" when it comes to prostitutes. Hopefully this Bill will not increase tolerance for rhino poachers either? Some vocations are simply anti-social.

Third, what about albinism? People cannot help it when they are born with certain features – physical or identity. But when black parents welcome a child with no skin pigment into the world, the issue of skin color really gets complicated. Albinos are not whites. They are white blacks. So to speak. They inevitably suffer from discrimination – and worse, they get it from both sides. The point is, *what is racism?* Is it only about skin color? Or is it connected to other terms in the list like "ethnic or social origin, color, culture and language"? In fact, two races can share one skin color, like Germans and Jews. Like waBantu and Nilotics. The Nuers of Sudan, Ethiopians and Somalis are Nilotics. That is a different race from the wabantu. Likewise the Ba Baroa, formerely known as "bushmen". They are non-whites too, but they are a different race from the waBantu. When the Khoisan are mistreated by either blacks or whites – it is racism.

Over a decade has passed since the *World Conference on Racism* – in 2003 in Durban. It came a whole decade after the end of apartheid. Obviously in the wake of Democracy's advent in South Africa this was the right place to seal political correctness on this topic with an international standard. Or was it? What about Rwanda? For in the years between the dawn of Democracy in South Africa and the Indaba at which a definitive global standard on Racism was agreed, came the Rwandan Genocide. Listen to one clause from the proceedings of that conference, which seems to have been inspired by this recognition: "*27. We express our concern that, beyond the fact that racism is gaining ground, contemporary forms and manifestations of racism and xenophobia are striving to regain political, moral and even legal recognition in many ways...*"

Legitimization of discrimination – in new and unfamiliar forms - is what we have to worry about. This lines up with the new notion of "liquid evil" – that evil no longer comes in the form of (solid) graven images or even (rational) ideologies, but just creeps in around your cherished convictions and values - almost undetected.

That's what happened in Rwanda. Hutus committed genocide against waTutsis. Both are blacks. But they are distinct races – Hutus are Bantu and the waTutsi are Nilotic. It is not racism when Zulus offend Xhosas, as they are both Bantus. That is tribalism. But if Sothos offend Khoisan, *that is racism*. So how is it that in a country with 11 national languages, these are all either Bantu or European tongues? What happened to the true vernacular? For the Ba Boroa were here long before the arrival of either blacks overland or whites by sea.

In Europe, the term "ethnic cleansing" reflects that when Christians offend Muslims it is ethnic or religious - not racist. But it WAS racism when Germans offended Jews BECAUSE they were distinct races (Arians and Semitics, to be exact). So when South African blacks (i.e. Bantus) loot and burn the shop of a Somalian (i.e. Nilotic) – that is racism. Why do we just call it xenophobia? Are we contending that blacks are never racist?

The case is often made by South Africans that when blacks offend whites, it is not racism. This does not line up with international standards. Xangans offending Pedis is tribalism. Or visa versa. South Africans offending Zimbabweans is xenophobia. Or visa versa. Whites offending blacks is racism. Or visa versa.

So when a columnist of Fred Khumalo's stature writes words like these, it rings of prejudice: *"The truth is, white people, there will be occasions where you will be singled out for your whiteness. For in the popular imagination, whiteness still represents privilege. But to burst your bubble: the majority of the people being singled out for victimization – through structural impoverishment, which leads to all manner of social ills – are black."*

The response in the opposite column in the Voices section of City Press came from Ernst Roets: *"The idea that black people are incapable of racism seems to gain ground among so-called progressive commentators. The claim is glaringly bankrupt of philosophical thought and can easily be refuted. My concern, however, is that those who make these claims appear to be too scared to have their views scrutinized, and therefore only respond to any criticism with intensified accusations of racism."*

I share this concern. Could this be one new manifestation of "liquid evil" creeping in? I often worry about affirmative action that favors the large majority. That trending is *positively* dangerous.

The public was invited to comment on the Bill. I made a contribution before the closing date of December 1st 2016. But it takes a very long time to get legislation like this to be approved by Parliament. Bills can languish for years in the National Assembly, before they become Acts.

My concern is that this Bill essentially targeted only murder, robbery (and housebreaking, assault, use of firearms, car-jacking), rape and arson. On the one hand, these are the manifestations that were witnessed during the Xenophobia outbreaks in 2008 and 2015. On the other hand, liquid evil will not necessarily recur in these same forms. Here are some scenarios of hate crimes that are never mentioned in the Bill:

- A foreigner receives a letter from his employer that accepts a resignation that he never submitted. The foreigner is literate, so the Law requires the employer to have a written resignation. But there isn't one. This ploy isolates the victim, who might have a case in a Labour court - but not if "the system" closes ranks with the employer
- The tenant's landlord is a foreigner. Better yet, the tenant works in government while the landlord's revenue is from

these rental incomes. The tenant stops paying rent and starts spreading a lot of false allegations about the landlord. This may be Defamation or even Crimen Injuria, but hatred is at the heart of it, judging by the jibes in related correspondence

- A foreigner owns a company that does business with government. He encounters some corruption and blows the whistle. For what he regards as good citizenship, he becomes the butt of innuendo and recriminations even the cancellation of standing government contracts. He tries to complain to government about unfair treatment, but even law enforcement is so porous that it is readily influenced by politicians and friends. If not totally "captured" like the NPA was. So expensive and time-consuming litigation is his only option

- (The Zulu king recently terminated payment of Lobola, so it would appear that even among national families, there are problems with the "monetization" of this custom.) But what about when a foreigner pays the Lobola for a local bride, only to find that he has been scammed by her family? His own family remains in a far-away country. So her family just pockets the money and starts looking for another foreigner to swindle. Traditional leaders close ranks with the bride, who lies through her teeth about the foreigner so her family can keep the loot. Cherished local custom has become the setting for entrapment

- When a white foreigner applies to Home Affairs for a Customary Marriage certificate, he is refused clearance by the Immigration officer, who states that these are only for "indigenous" people. When he reports that to the SAPS precinct, he finds that she has relatives who are policemen working there. When he speaks to the Social Worker, he is confronted for allegedly marrying a national "to get his citizenship" – an outright lie - as he had already obtained his non-res ID book before marrying her. Innuendo becomes full-blown gaslighting

- When a white foreign man marries a younger black woman, local black men take exception that foreigners are "stealing their women", and do not back off. Her male friends relentlessly continue to phone and visit her - even at her new home. They can speak to her in a language that the groom doesn't understand. When she visits her parents' home they re-emerge as suitors and lovers, in a country with 7.5 million sero-positive citizens, who should know from public health awareness-raising that the biggest risk of them all is "multiple sexual partners". When he asks the SAPS precinct for intervention, he is told that they only deal with crime, not with domestic matters

Not one of these cases is imaginary. They have all been reported in real life. In the past four years. The police and prosecutors responded to none of the above, they just buried the cases.

Behind the view that what blacks do to whites may be crime - but cannot be racism – is the history of structural racism. Specifically, of grand apartheid. In Germany too, extermination of Jews was not just bad behavior – it was detrimental government policy. The same was true of "ethnic cleansing" in the Balkans. So I think the argument goes something like this – whites systematically exploited blacks and that legacy continues "through structural impoverishment" to use Fred Khumalo's phrase. So it cannot be turned around the other way.

Really? So when a South African loots and burns a Somali's shop, a foreigner who is outnumbered, who may not speak the vernacular, and who may have legitimate political asylum in South Africa – it's not racism? I think it is. Just because there are wider definitions of "hate-crime" does not mean that black South Africans can excuse themselves from racism.

Racism does not have to be systemic to be racism. It can be a random act that one person commits, or even just an attitude, a comment. But when families organize themselves to swindle foreigners of Lobola and the traditional structures and even Home Affairs close ranks to protect the perpetrators and to isolate the victim, then it is either a lynch mob or even racketeering. Not just one act of one person, but not yet structural as in the case of apartheid. Somewhere is the middle. These are hate crimes. And they are organized crimes. But blacks tend to excuse themselves, and to blame everything on Apartheid. They do this on automatic pilot.

Is it inconceivable that two black South Africans would force a Somalian into a coffin? Not in the light of what we have seen from time to time in the Xenophobia outbreaks. That would also be racism. As was the Rwandan genocide, when liquid evil flooded African streets and villages on an unprecedented scale. With no whites to blame. In fact, it was the white Canadian General posted in Rwanda commanding the "blue helmets" who pleaded with the black Secretary General of the United Nations for more resources to protect the waTutsi from Hutu hate-crimes. He did not succeed in getting the extra support he needed, so thousands of African people were slaughtered – by other African people.

Is it true that zebras can only see in black and white?!

6. Is "Implicit Bias" the new term for "Closed Racism"?

I have spent many years working in Angola and Mozambique. These were colonized by the Portuguese, who were trying to establish an east-west belt across Africa, in the infamous "scramble for Africa". But they ran headlong into the British at the Council of Berlin, who wanted to build a Cape-to-Cairo railroad, much like the railways that they were building at the same time across North America, to stimulate development and trade. Their version of "progress".

My lusophone friends tell me that the British and Dutch practiced "open racism". That is, they separated whites and blacks into their respective areas. To their way of thinking, this gave at least a modicum of respect to the blacks. Whereas the Portuguese practiced "assimilation". Blacks could become Portuguese citizens if they learned to speak the language well, if they converted to Catholicism, if they wore a suit and a tie, if they learned "table manners", etc. At first this might look like an absence of the attitude of white supremacy, but the lusophones say that what it really meant was that *there was NO VALUE in local culture and in traditional customs*. This, they say, was "closed racism". It was even more arrogant than "open racism".

What is amazing is that whites succeeded in putting this over on black "assimilados", in a context where they were a small minority – greatly outnumbered in terms of demographics. That is, in their African colonies. But of course when the "assimilados" visited Portugal, they were the ones who were out-numbered there. They were stricken with awesome Europe, and even guns had to be demystified before armed struggles could get underway. Superior fire-power kept the white minority dominating the black majority. The demystification of the gun and arming blacks were important steps on the road to *Uhuru* and *Amandla* (freedom and power). In short, to Democracy.

Only recently, since the 1990s, psychologists have been studying a phenomenon called "implicit bias" – as distinct from "explicit bias". It is not hard to detect "explicit bias" – the manifestations of behavior that keep one class, gender or race with hegemony over the others. Men have their ways of perpetuating their advantage over women. Aristocrats have always had ways of maintaining their supremacy over the "hoi polio". White colonists and settlers ("boers" in South Africa) still have their ways of keeping a "hedge" against black supremacy.

Children and youth who grew up in a racist system learned from these explicit biases. In South Africa, there were not only men's toilets and women' toilets, but also white men's toilets and black men's toilets. Separating men and women did not serve as much to keep the advantage for men, surely. Because the numbers - when it comes to gender - are roughly equal.

But the serfs always out-numbered the barons and the blacks have always out-numbered the whites, in Africa. Hitler had it relatively easy - hegemony is much easier to sustain when you are in the majority. The Nazi's brought the Darwinian doctrine of survival of the fittest into it. They bought into "Social Darwinism" as opposed to either "Socialism" or "Liberalism". From this evolved their notion of the superior or master race. This was not unlike the warped Calvinist theology of the Afrikaners – that they were God's chosen people and would gradually take control of Africa. That did not pan out, either. Both were deeply mistaken doctrines.

It is hard to hang on to hegemony when the demographics are against you. FW de Klerk realized that, and called it "unsustainable".

In America, this is where it gets nasty. If you ever wondered how juries there acquit policemen for shooting innocent young blacks, think about "implicit memories" and "implicit bias".

You cannot remember "implicit memories", they have just embedded themselves in you deeply. Past experiences do not come back to consciousness level, but they nevertheless influence you. Maybe the way that bureaucracy has weighed you down so often makes you hate red tape and filling out forms? This is a subliminal thing. Or a scare you got as a child – that you cannot even remember - still makes you timid around dogs?

Transfer this kind of attitudinal reality to members of a jury. In America, most of them will be white because whites outnumber blacks there ten-to-one. So nine out of ten jury members probably see things pretty much the way white cops do. Call it an empathy. Ken Wytsma, the author of The Myth of Equality, puts it like this:

"Those who clamor for justice after unarmed shootings are not declaring the shooter guilty and demanding a sentence. Rather, they are demanding that over time in an open environment, the process go far enough that any implicit bias at work can be exposed and addressed. They simply desire that the system work well enough to allow us to confidently declare that in the end, whether there's a sentence or not, justice has been done. This doesn't mean every police shooting should go to an open trial or that every grand jury is wrong; it simply means we need to acknowledge the role implicit racial bias can play in a closed-room hearing that doesn't require a unanimous conclusion. And we need to ensure that the law is actually blind – remember the classical statue of blindfolded Lady Justice holding balanced scales?"

Could it be that all the long delays in bringing perpetrators of State Capture to justice in South Africa is another manifestation of "implicit memories"? There are so many horrible ways that blacks were treated, and so many cruel whites, albeit in the minority, that blacks are finding it hard to convict and sentence one another now? Call it an empathy, embedded in a communal culture. Black prosecutors and black judges trying to dispense justice from a system that was originally set up so that a white minority could maintain its hegemony over a black majority. Surely this is why intentional efforts were made to close the Scorpions and to capture the NPA?

The Treason Trialists were political prisoners, not criminals. They were sequestered by white supremacists, on Robben Island. But Lady Justice kept her blindfold on, and after a long, long wait, they were released. Thanks to a huge weight of eternal pressure on the system.

Now it's the turn of black prosecutors and black judges to condemn black leaders for corruption and patronage. Yes, they broke the law. Yes, they looted and plundered. Yes, the proportions of it are so huge that they have brought the country to its knees economically, and into disrepute.

But there is this implicit bias that kicks in. It says "That man was once our President", or (fatalistically) "We will end up putting half of the Cabinet and the NEC in jail". How can they bring themselves to do that? "Everyone has some smallanyana skeletons in their closet."

Like closed racism, it rather puts the Judicial System in a bad light. It makes the Prosecutors look like "impimpi" and the Judges look like "coconuts".

Communal culture is now running institutions set up to serve Individualism. Implicit memories are getting in the way of explicit evidence. Blacks outnumber whites ten-to-one, so it is only to be expected that those implicit biases are holding sway. It may be subliminal, not even conscious, but only one out of three cases opened by the police is ever prosecuted. And watch the Stalingrad defense strategies kick in on that one case that is prosecuted! Trials take forever, being punted and remanded time and again. This is not about human rights, it is way deeper than that. It is a deep suspicion or even rejection of the Judicial System, like the move to withdraw from the ICC was – an institution that was set up to try to keep people's democratic hopes from being trampled down by dictators. Why would a Democracy withdraw from the ICC?! The rationale was that it was allegedly being used to target African rulers. Is that true? Or is it "implicit bias"?

Just as blacks in America are shocked to see juries acquit white policemen for shooting blacks, whites in South Africa are aghast that perpetrators of corruption and patronage continue to enjoy impunity. And for all the same reasons. The Judicial System is not compensating for implicit bias. The law is not blind. And as blacks and whites are equal, can blacks not have racist attitudes towards whites as well? That combined with the prevailing demographics could prove to get very nasty.

1. Affirmative Action is aggravating Implicit Bias

Performance and quality are two different things.

Our new NDPP Shamila Batohi reports that the NPA has an overall 93 percent conviction rate. Those are high marks.

But put this statistic together with another one – from Bheki Cele's report earlier the same year. Only one out of three crimes reported ever gets prosecuted. That means that if the police will even open a case when you report a crime (and they have been known to refuse to do so), they may not ever find "proof". So when the police dockets are full of gaps, the prosecutors won't touch them. They devolve them to the police. Many of these cases die on the vine, so to speak.

If you take the NPA results another way – as a percentage of cases opened by the police – it is much lower. 93 percent of just one-third of the cases opened by the police is a mere 31 percent. The truth probably lies somewhere between these two extremes. Results are inflated when prosecutors can simply walk away from their civic responsibility.

Separating the SAPS (investigation) from the NPA (prosecution) created the conditions for high crime rates in general and State Capture in particular. This is why they closed the Scorpions, which could both investigate and prosecute. And it is why the new President granted Shamila Batohi her proviso that the NPA can have its own investigative unit.

Screening at entry level is key to making the statistics look as good as possible. The police have been known to refuse to open dockets for cases that look un-winnable when reported. For example, where it might be almost impossible to trace any evidence. Instead, they might just promise to look into it, without granting you a case number or investigating officer. This is not really "rigging" but it does tweak the statistics in favour of the police.

There is another hidden anomaly that makes rejecting cases easy for the police. If they don't register a case at all, it can often be because of a combination of "implicit bias" and "affirmative action". If not due to political interference, or outright fear of the mafia.

Implicit Bias is embedded in the base population. For example, when you hear of a mainly white jury in the USA convicting a young black man for murder, when he claims innocence, there is almost always some degree of implicit bias at play. By "implicit" we are talking about the attitudes, the beliefs and the prejudices of the jury members. In the USA, nine out of ten people are white. So when it comes to jury duty, they will always call more whites than blacks. But this has a detrimental influence on jury decisions.

Juries listen to the explicit arguments and look at the explicit evidence – witnesses, photos, documents, etc. But no one can make a decision even in the face of hard evidence that is free of "implicit bias" – the attitudes, beliefs and prejudices that you carry into the court room, embedded deeply in your psyche. This explains the "fear factor" – why so often innocent young black men are unjustly convinced for crimes by predominantly white juries. This is "implicit bias".

But in the USA, affirmative action favours minorities – like blacks. So it runs in the opposite direction from implicit bias. The whole idea of affirmative action is to counter the tendencies of the majority.

Except for South Africa, where affirmative action favours the majority. Now you get implicit bias running in the same direction as affirmative action! For whites, and especially white men, this is double jeopardy.

I have been turned away more than once at the Reception desk of my local SAPS precinct. The rejection is palpable – the police want to screen out un-winnable cases, so it starts at entry level. They will just not even open a docket. Not surprisingly, I tend to be better received by white policemen, especially by white men, on the rare occasion that they are working at Reception.

Most of those attending are black, as are most of the members of the public lining up to be attended. Blacks are equally human to whites – so they also have embedded attitudes, beliefs and prejudices. We may not have jury duty in South Africa, but it plays out another way. The slogan "Justice for all" gets eroded by this double-whammy of implicit bias running in the same direction as affirmative action. It is close to sheer Triumphalism.

In the name of "screening" they can play unfair with other citizens and residents. Even assuming that they are all generally honest people. I believe that some are.

But I also read the newspapers. It's pretty obvious that there are some dishonest people in the ranks of the police as well. But that is another story, for news reporters, not for mere Op-Ed columnists like me.

Your basic, honest policewoman or man cannot escape their own "implicit bias". We vilify it when a black youth gets unjustly convicted by a white jury in the USA. But we don't confess that all people have implicit bias – black and white. Worse yet, we in South Africa synergize implicit bias with affirmative action, when they should be containing one another.

The result is that screening is done unevenly and that not even the baseline three cases that Bheki Cele reports accurately encompass a lot of crime that has been committed in this country. A lot of it never even gets registered, even when reported to the police. It is weeded out in order to make the statistics presented to Parliament look as good as possible. But Justice has not been served. Lady Justice peaked from behind her blindfold.

8. Out of Apartheid; into a de facto Two State Solution

I thought of the lament "Out of the frying pan and into the fire" when I read about a speech by FW de Klerk. He had tried to avert an unsustainable future but he is now asking questions about the sustainability of a new form of Racism. Elsewhere known as Black Supremacy.

In fact, The Economist has often pointed out that when Minority-rule dominates the majority, especially if that is by force, it is unsustainable. But when affirmative action favours the Majority, then you are on the edge of something more sinister, going down the road to intolerance. The white Germans did it to the white Jews; and the black Hutus did it to the black Tutsis. It does not have to be across the colour bar.

Looking at a map of Israel with the Palestinian Authority inside it is not so very different from looking at an apartheid atlas of South Africa. Except that in Israel there are only two states, not many Bantustans within one large country. One operates inside the other, but that "Two State Solution" is not in vogue any more. For it does not sit well with a line of thinking and a global value system that generally promotes inclusion, equality and harmonization.

But is South Africa really moving towards a melting-pot model like Brazil, where there is plenty of racial mixing even at the beach – not just on TV?

There are still extremes in South Africa – like the deep rural areas of the Eastern Cape which remain very traditional. And on the opposite extreme – Orania in the Northern Cape.

Take one photo of a segregated classroom and you could lose your job! Although that teacher fought back and proved that she had every right to make that photo public. Because citizens have a right to know.

I just think that we are hiding what really happens. South Africa is polarizing – as are many countries. But here, the proportions get scary. Whites almost need the wealth advantage – to counterbalance the fact that they are significantly outnumbered – by a hostile crowd.

What will happen to the whites if that epicentre of wealth shifts suddenly? It would have the same effect that "load shift" has on cargo transport. It could up-end the equilibrium. Those boats crossing the Mediterranean might suddenly be filled with whites looking for a port of entry into Europe, instead of blacks.

This sounds a bit crazy, but within one week I have read a brilliant article in the Daily Maverick about the rising influence of the Alt Right in the world – including South Africa (by Miriame Thamm), and also received a bulletin from Abahlali Press about the government's recent deployment of a new generation of "Casspirs" to conduct military repression of the surge for land being guided by Abahlali baseMjondolo. Land and Dignity. Is this one and the same country?!

What about language? Tshwane University recently decided to adopt English as its medium of instruction. How did that make white voters feel about the future of their country? In the attempt to unify people, that will actually have a polarizing effect, alienating whites. I agree with Tito Mboweni that we will regret this 30 years from now. This could be why the Freedom Front Plus enjoyed a surge of support in the 2019 elections, after languishing among the small parties for over a decade. It is now clearly on the up and up, representing the Alt Right.

While support on the Left seems to be converging on the EFF, which rose from 25 seats to 44 seats. That is an increase of 19 seats. Exactly the same number of seats that the ANC lost. The two big parties (ANC and DA) are shrinking. Support is polarizing to smaller parties like the the FF+ and the EFF. Can the centre really hold? Do voters see the DA as just an "ANC-light"?

What about land expropriation without compensation as a policy, on its way towards legislation? Yes it will benefit blacks in terms of dignity and level the playing field in term of access to the means of production. But it also will bend property rights to the breaking point, having a knock-on effect on the rule of law, and even on our baseline of non-racialism. What is it doing to social cohesion?

In Israel, the Two State Solution basically divides one space into two zones. Just before the United Nations was established, the British adopted a similar Two State Solution for India. Move the Muslims to Pakistan (West and East, the latter became Bangladesh at a later date) and concentrate the Hindus in the middle. They called it "Partition". It seemed to be working until Hindu nationalism started to boil over under Modi.

But when decades later, Myanmar tries a similar approach – ringfencing Muslims into an enclave and sequestering them onto an island for from Buddhist shores – that has raised some eyebrows. Sometimes Myanmar has been accused of "Genocide" - for all the same reasons that so many champion the cause of the Palestinians. The Two State Solution is no longer regarded as a goal, just a stage of development as history evolves.

In that part of the world, the Levant, policy has been changing for millennia. Xerxes was a centralizer who brought the elite of the nations he conquered back to his capital at Suza. But his son Art Xerxes reversed that, even helping his Minister of Security (Nehemiah) to rebuild the walls of Jerusalem – a security project. A wall. It created the conditions for the city's economy to revive and flourish again.

Later the Roman Emperor Hadrian built a wall – across the northern frontier of his empire – to manage the incursions of Picts and Scots, into Britain. The Chinese also built a wall along their northern border, to manage the raiding Mongols. But the Democrats are now calling Donald Trump's plan to build a border wall "a fifth century solution to a twenty-first century problem". There goes the polarization again.

Those photos taken by Johnny Miller from his drones are so graphic – nice suburbs on one side of the wall with their glistening swimming pools. On the other side of the wall, townships of grinding poverty. We live in a de facto Two State Solution.

But as the rhetoric gets more radical, and the on-going job shrinkage continues because investors are scared away... as crime levels rise because most of the police are intimate with the majority and not inclined to risk their lives to protect a white minority... as the fear of gangsters begins to surpass the fear of law enforcement... the Two State Solution is taking hold. Here it is not just a phase, it is becoming a destination.

Yet the tectonic plates of world politics are shifting. America is more focused on patriotism than on policing the world. Bolsanaro is rocking Brazil and with it BRICS, just like Trump rocked America first and then NATO. Brexit has rocked Europe, which could spell the exit of Northern Ireland and maybe Scotland from the UK. This new Alt Right trending is rocking Venezuela as never before. A lot of this, believe it or not, has to do with slowing down the migration flows. When Trump says "make America great again" he means in part applying the brakes on immigration and not letting Spanish challenge English as the lingua franca. America is supposed to be a melting pot, not a Two-State Solution. English was chosen by Congress, and intentionally so. (It won over German by only one vote – in the US Congress that still met in Pennsylvania, before Washington was built.)

With our voices, we reject a Two State Solution for Israel and Palestine. But with our policies and practices we are entrenching it in South Africa by polarizing citizens. In a word, this is hypocrisy. We put the "quick wins" before a strategic commitment to social cohesion and non-racialism.

What the ANC calls "unity" is not that at all, it is a strategy to avert the decline of the radical Left in the context of a global boom in Conservatism. Neither faction of the ANC can possibly win an election any more – so they need one another and thus they awkwardly stick together. This is a kind of gridlock. They are not unified – they are clinging to one another for dear life! South Africa takes sides with Maduro in Venezuela, risking further alienation from the North, whose economies have been growing while Venezuela, Zimbabwe and North Korea have been sinking.

This kind of thinking will not take us past our own Two State Solution, because it probably cannot see that this is where we have ended up. Out of the frying pan, and into the fire.

9. From Hardened Attitudes to Balkanization

The Balkans have seen the futility of confrontation since the mists of pre-History, when the Greeks tried and failed to conquer Troy.

So there are many enclaves that still remain in the Balkans. Armies have criss-crossed this area, not just for centuries but for millennia. Out of Macedonia came Alexander the Great, crossing the Dardanelles on his way to conquer the known world. The Ottoman Turk empire invaded Europe and occupied some of the Balkans, but failed to take Vienna.

St Paul heard a "Macedonian call" from the south/east shores of the Dardanelles, and went on to evangelize Europe. The Huns invaded from Asia and established Hungary. Centuries later, Islam challenged the Eastern Empire (of Rome), long after the Western Empire had crumbled. So you get pockets of Muslims still living in the Balkans, among both Catholic and Orthodox Christians. Predominantly Christian to the north and west, predominantly Muslim to the south and east, it has even bequeathed the word "balkanized" to the English language.

The name derives from the Balkan Mountains, but "balkanization" has become a pejorative term for political and social melt-down. Both the Kingdom of Yugoslavia and Czechoslovakia of the 20th century have disappeared. The Czechs and the Slovaks got a divorce, and Yugoslavia blew apart into Serbia, Montenegro, Kosovo, Croatia, Slovenia, Bosnia and Herzegovina. There was a political earthquake of sorts.

More recently, and not far away along the coast of the Black Sea, the Russians have annexed Crimea. Technically, it belongs to the Ukraine, but this peninsula had become predominantly Russian over time. A bridge has recently been built to joint it to the Russian mainland. That was an act of Russian expansionism, of aggression, which may contain in it a kernel of self-determination - by the occupants of Crimea?

Another Mediterranean story is also brewing in Catalonia. There has been a popular movement there, with deep historical roots, for this province to separate from Spain. A dozen or so of the leaders of this movement were put on trial in Madrid – for sedition. Back in Roman times, Catalonia was a prosperous province of Rome. It has a long and proud history as a region and culture. So when Barcelona play Madrid in soccer, the feelings run deeper than sport.

At the other end of the Mediterranean, on its African (south) shores, Eritrea succeeded in seceding from Ethiopia. It has become a country, which soon after ended up in an ugly border-war with Ethiopia. However, after a 10-year wait, that dispute has been settled and peace has broken out.

Not far from there, in the Levant, the Two-State Solution of the Palestinian Authority inside Israel is percolating away. This has been mentioned in the previous chapter. For South Africa seems to be evolving into a similar scenario – a dominant state with at least one vigorous minority, sharing the same space.

Scotland has a secessionist party that is even represented in British Parliament. But its popularity has mostly remained a minority, even inside Scotland. Then along came Brexit, with the United Kingdom (which includes Scotland) leaving the European Union. Scotland is opposed, and wants to re-join in the EU in its own right. The reunification of Ireland could be on the cards?

The biggest challenge to "getting Brexit done" was the border between Ireland and Northern Ireland. A century ago, the first shots were fired in Ireland's liberation struggle. Eventually, the southern part of the island gained its independence, leaving the northern province of Ulster inside the UK. The north had a much higher density of "settlers" than the rest of the island. But there is now talk that Brexit may have created the conditions for reunification?

These are times of uncertainty. But they are also dangerous times. Explosive situations. It was breath-taking to see the reunification of Germany after decades of Cold War.

The American Civil War is usually remembered for the liberation of slaves. But it started over states' rights. When one state after another in the South started to secede from the Union, this was treated as treason. So the states that had seceded formed a Confederacy and took on the North in a military confrontation. The celebrated Confederate general, Robert E Lee, was personally against slavery and had never owned slaves. But he believed that states should be governed by those living within them and fought against a model of Union that denied this state sovereignty.

To the north of the states of the Union is the province of Quebec in Canada. Since the forces of the British general Wolfe defeated the French general Montcalm at the battle of the Plains of Abraham, Quebec has been part of Canada. But it had started as an independent French colony, and continues to have aspirations that Quebecers call "Sovereignty Association".

There are lessons in all these secessionist models for South Africa, where attitudes are hardening. First, there is some danger lurking in Zulu nationalism. This is by far the biggest of a dozen main tribes in the country, with a proud history and culture of its own. For one thing, particularly in the ruling alliance, there is rising resentment over the way the fourth State President was sidelined. (He is a Zulu.) And he now faces corruption charges in the State Capture saga. This matter must be treated with the utmost wisdom and discretion. One of its complicating factors is Zulu nationalism. In the 2019 elections, there was a resurgence of support for the Inkatha Freedom party. Its leader is one of the arch-critics of Zuma and the ANC. So this gets complicated. Because while that was a setback for the ruling party, it shows that Zulu nationalism is still a force to be reckoned with.

Secondly, attitudes of Black Supremacy that manifest in policies like affirmative action and the expropriation of land without compensation could trigger a stand-off. For example, there has been talk of a tax boycott, at a time when tax revenue has been sagging while Treasury officials concentrated on looting. It became a place of self-service, not of public service.

One thing is for sure, history moves on and borders and Constitutions are dynamic, not static. In Southern Africa, there are already enclave countries like Lesotho and eSwatini. Not to mention Botswana which is also dominated by one tribe. No country is immune to change, especially as Donald Trump has moved the emphasis of politics from Globalism to Patriotism. For several decades, Regional Integration has been the mantra of politics, so this shift to Patriotism could prove to be a game-changer. The Covid-19 pandemic caused borders to close and countries to dispute over scarce medical and financial resources. It showed that nationalism still a force to be reckoned with.

Who would have thought? That when a black president moved into the White House, that by the end of his second term, the doctrine of Inclusion would have reached the epic proportions it did? For example, anyone who was uncertain of their own sexual orientation could use either a Men's room or a Women's room.

So who would have thought that the very next president would be elected for running on a platform to erect a wall along the southern border of the USA? Some see this as radical exclusion. Others see it as plain law enforcement. But it has polarized a country – not as much as under Abraham Lincoln, but this has happened very fast. Like Brexit, it seems to be running in the opposite direction that history has been moving in. It was a rebuke to those who thought that they knew better, so they took minorities for granted. Even when Conservatives are not in power, it does not mean that they are defeated. Or that they have lost their courage, identity and purpose.

This is what Canadian historian Lord Conrad Black means when he writes that *"America's resurgence is reshaping the world"*. Donald Trump found it hard to finance and build his monument to Isolationism. However, because he kept this topic on the front burner, his border wall has started to take shape. It is only half physical, but equally metaphorical. The tide of Mexican immigration has fallen drastically. Over a million illegal immigrants have been identified, picked up, and repatriated. The flow into the USA has decreased to a trickle.

South Africa should re-think its strategy, starting with its assumptions. The external environment of Opportunities (external positives) and Threats (external negatives) is changing. China's economy was already slowing down, even before it took the knock of the Covid-19 pandemic. Brazil elected Bolsanaro, so BRICS will be undergoing some changes. Venezuela is under pressure from many sides – Latin America, North America and Europe – to recover its misplaced democratic routines. This has put is main sponsor Cuba into a vice, economically speaking.

South Africa's internals – its Strengths (internal positives) and Weaknesses (internal negatives) – are also changing. Eskom is only one of several state-owned enterprises that has been chronically failing, but the proportions of the power utility's slide constitute a major risk to an economy already in recession. Crime, corruption and patronage have reached mad proportions, depleting the Treasury. Tax revenue was down, even before the Covid-19 tsunami hit our economy. The 2019 elections illuminated a disgust with the lack of any enticing choices.

The Electorate withdrew its democratic support, because more people didn't bother to even register or to vote once registered, than the number of citizens who voted. This was a statement. It was withdrawal of consent. And when the results were tabulated of those who did vote, the ruling party's majority shrank significantly. It was a rebuke.

Both its Leftist flank and also the Alt Right enjoyed significant increases in support. There is a polarization happening, that is best visualized in the mapping of results that can be found in the Preamble to this book.

Is this the time for attitudes to harden into alienation and even hatred? Is there no way that blacks can park their bitterness and whites can park their fear? Social and cultural polarization historically lead to political balkanization. Given a few extra ingredients as catalysts, this can lead to conflict and divorce. Finance Minister Tito Mboweni made the comment, upon hearing that the University of Pretoria has dropped Afrikaans language and will now use only English as the medium of instruction, that this would be regretted "thirty years from now". Yes, the chickens will always come home to roost.

I have lived long enough now to watch history repeating itself. History is not only lineal, going forward, it is also cyclical. What goes around, comes around.

Those who grew up with black-and-white television have been found to often dream in black and white. Are we losing our capacity to dream in colour – of a Rainbow Nation?

10. How Not to Impair the Dignity of Fellow Citizens

Non-racialism is still under excruciating pressure in South Africa. Close to home, I noticed this back in 2016 when two incidents happened in Belfast. Those were described in the opening chapter of this book.

Then in early 2017, there were two more incidents in the news. These were mentioned in the second chapter. I purposely try to present these incidents in pairs, to show that attitudes have hardened on both sides. I try not to point the finger at one side or the other, but at both.

In the news, infamous names come to mind on both sides...

Estate agent Penny Sparrow was fined R150 000 by the Umzinto Equality Court for her racist rant on a FaceBook post. She had described black beachgoers as "monkeys".

Then former Idols SA judge Gareth Cliff found himself in hot water after he tweeted about this uproar. A deluge of responses labeled him a racist and demanded his removal as an Idols judge.

Estate agent Vicki Momberg went on a racist rant shortly after being a victim of a smash-and-grab in Johannesburg in 2016. She loosely hurled the k-word 48 times at police officers and 10111 operators who had tried to assist following her ordeal. Her tirade was caught on camera and the video soon went viral. This has landed her in jail – she was sentenced to two years' imprisonment by the Randburg Magistrate's Court.

In early 2018, Mark Lamberti resigned from both his board positions - on Business Leadership South Africa and Eskom. The North Gauteng High court found that he had impaired the dignity of Adila Chowan, a former employee at Associated Motor Holdings, an Imperial Holdings subsidiary. This followed him referring to Chowan as a "female, employment equity candidate", a remark that Lamberti later apologised for.

On the other side of the racial divide there are also indiscretions...

Judge Nkola Motata was recorded swearing at onlookers after he crashed his Jaguar into a wall. He used the word "boer" to refer to Richard Baird, a key state witness who captured the cell phone footage and recordings of Motata angrily admonishing him and two female Metro police officers. A JSC tribunal concluded that his racist comments – and the dishonest way he conducted his trial – could justify his removal as a judge.

SANDF Major Mohlala reacted to a photo on social media of a badly beaten 80-year-old white man saying that the attackers "should actually have poked out his eyes and tongue so that the last people he would ever see, were the killers and he could go to his grave with the nightmare." He went on: "Apartheid is in him. All of these old white people think we are stupid when they say they were opposed to apartheid. We will not forget what they have done. *Now it is the white people's turn.*"

According to the SAHRC: "There is no justification for such hateful commentary by any South African. Given the position held by Major Mohlala in the SANDF, these remarks are simply unacceptable."

In another case, the SAHRC was granted an order that interdicts and restrains Edward Zuma from "publishing, propagating, advocating or communicating hate speech", following statements he made in 2017 – about Pravin Gordhan and Derek Hanekom. The order forms part of a settlement reached between the oldest son of former president Jacob Zuma and the SAHRC at the Durban Equality Court.

And in mid-2018, editor Ferial Haffajee sued columnist Eric Miyeni for describing her as a "black snake in the grass, deployed by white capital to sow discord among blacks". According to journalist Max du Preez, this was definitely hate-speech. Especially the part of her working for white masters.

In a tweet on July 25th 2019, ex-President Jacob Zuma referred to Derek Hanekom as a "known enemy agent". Zuma was reacting to EFF leader Julius Malema's claims that Hanekom had conspired with the party to oust him via a motion of no confidence in the National Assembly. Hanekom sued him for Defamation and won. Hanekom's lawyers said to call someone who fought for liberation an apartheid government spy was defamatory, false and had caused significant harm to his reputation. It was pure gaslighting.

A black and white Rainbow

What ever happened to the Rainbow Nation? It seems that we are regressing from Technicolor back to the age of black and white. This does not bode well for the non-racialism project. Especially when politicians like Julius Malema and Blade Nzimande seem to get away with it. In 2018, Malema said that he was going to remove Mayor Trollip "because he is white". In 2017, Nzimande publicly called Michael Sun, a member of the Joburg Mayoral Committee, a "fong kong" who was knowledgeable in "karate". How and why do politicians get away with this kind of hate-speech?

With elections only months away, Malema was acquitted of hate-speech for various comments he had made on the campaign trail. However, he did not get off without a rebuke. It would be good for politicians not to be exempt from impairing the dignity of fellow citizens. If anything, they should be held up as the role-models, and held to an even higher standard.

Ashwen Willemse walked off the set of a Super Sports show, objecting to his being patronized and treated as a "quota" by his co-panelists Mallet and Botha. Eventually, all three of them were suspended for their inability to sort out their differences amicably.

This litany of episodes is instructive. Inflammatory language like "monkeys, kaffirs, boers, fong kong, snakes" should be avoided – *always*.

Calling someone an equity employment candidate or even treating them as "quota" can provoke conflict. If you think that affirmative action is not helping - and maybe even hindering - then play the ball – not the man!

On the whole - although media coverage has never been impartial or balanced (neither historically nor in the present) - the Judiciary does seem to be refereeing the episodes fairly. As in the political arena, the Judiciary and Section 9 institutions like the SAHRC are proving to be our ethical and equitable anchor in the social sphere. It is important that court decisions serve as deterrents, which has been our purpose in cataloguing all these episodes above. Live and learn.

11. Forget Anger Management, we need Greed Therapy

Greed is a perennial human condition, with diverse manifestations. Siddhārtha Gautama a k a the Buddha's message was aimed at curbing craving. He prescribed meditation, introspection, self-denial, even asceticism – to try to beat the tendency to cling to material wealth, so as to reach the state of *nirvana*. This is a kind of rebirth or *karma*, the exact opposite to Madonna's *Material Girl*. Buddhist theology says that craving is the deepest hindrance to enlightenment.

In fact, some psychologists also regard greed as the ultimate addiction. Like the famous story about the multi-millionaire, who was asked why he didn't stop working, now that he had more wealth than he would ever need. His reply was: "I will. But just one more million first."

That resonates with the movie *The Wolf of Wall Street*, which was based on a true story. Greed came to possess Jordan's soul. You can watch his personality change as he becomes richer. He loses touch and makes outrageous decisions which bring about his own demise. How can vastly wealthy people be driven by a sense that smacks of deprivation or lacking? Is this deception or self-deception? It didn't fool Bob Dylan who wrote the song *A Satisfied Mind*:

Once I was wadding in fortune and fame

Everything that I dreamed of to get a start in life's game

But suddenly it happened

I lost every dime

But I'm richer by far with a satisfied mind.

This condition is sometimes called Affluenza, because affluence does not satisfy greed. Affluence begets greed. Greed outgrows the survival instinct or even the profit motive, and becomes avarice. You start to covet your neighbour's goods! And maybe even your neighbour's wife? The question that comes to mind is the extent to which this condition is at the root of Inequality, the rich-getting-richer-and-the-poor-getting-poorer syndrome, the widening wealth gap, the Gini coefficient, economic apartheid, etc.?

So when Afriforum worries that South Africa's food security could be shaken if land is confiscated from the Boers - because of their phenomenal success as farmers - it rings a bit hollow. Johnny Miller's contrasting images, taken from a hovering drone, are just too graphic. They bring to mind what Dorothy Day said about the role of nonprofits: *"To comfort the afflicted, and to afflict the comfortable"*.

Of course no one resists any opportunity to be seen in the role of comforting the afflicted. But who is ready to afflict the comfortable? Here are a few manifestations that could be driven by excessive greed:

First, the carpet-baggers of State Capture. They ripped off the public purse. They ignored the rules and gouged the Treasury so that they could feather their own nests. The Zondo Commission is unpacking the mechanics of it, and trying to proscribe the extent of it. (The latest estimates are trillions of Rand lost just during Zuma's second term as President.) The question here is about the bent spirituality that underpins such looting. What happened to *doing unto others as you would have them do unto you*?

Second, what about the enclave of rich whites that persists in a country where poor blacks outnumber them hugely. Isn't that as short-sighted as the Wolf of Wall Street? It is unsustainable and thus Land Reform is one of the obvious imperatives. As are cleaning up corruption and patronage, among others. There is no panacea, but a recipe of several ingredients. But really, someone has to afflict these comfortable citizens before we have a re-run of the French Revolution. Bye-bye Marie Antoinette. Hello Freedom, Equality, and Justice!

Third, confiscating people's land without any compensation is yet another manifestation of greed. Seriously, how does anyone square that approach with constitutional property rights and the deal that was reached to avert Civil War at CODESA? Pushing that button could well bring havoc down on the beloved country. Certainly in economic terms and maybe in para-military terms as well? These realities are reflected in the threats that a Boer defiantly posted on Facebook of the steps that he will take if his land is expropriated, and the specter of Julius Malema shooting off an AK47 from the stage of an EFF rally. Both of these extremes were ill-conceived. Shame on both of them.

One of the commonalities that binds South African citizens together is the high proportion of Christians on both sides of the racial divide and also on both sides of the wealth gap. Then you also have Muslim and Jewish citizens who agree with Christians that the Old Testament is "a lamp to our feet and a light to our path". They revere many patriarchs as prophets. On this note, the *Year of Jubilee* could shed some useful guidance on the issue of redistributing overall wealth and land in particular.

A pastor called Ron Sider published a book in 1978 called <u>Rich Christians in an Age of Hunger</u>. For many believers, it was a wake-up call, a kind of Greed Therapy. But he was a pastor, not an economist, and way out of his depth. His tendencies were very socialistic, as this was still a decade before the Berlin Wall came down, before Socialism was largely discredited. When the Communist Bloc all but disappeared, leaving only a remnant composed of North Korea, Zimbabwe, Cuba and Venezuela.

Meanwhile a response to his book was written by David Chilton called Productive Christians in an Age of Guilt-manipulators, in 1981. Chilton is another Christian author, but he disagreed sharply with Sider. In the following decade, the cutting edge of compassionate ministries moved from distributing free food aid to dispensing micro-loans – giving the poor "a hand up instead of a hand out".

Specifically, their takes on the Year of Jubilee differed immensely. Sider called for a Year of Jubilee in which wealthy Christians mostly in the North would give away massive resources into a redistribution mechanism, to level the playing field with the South. (A kind of religious Marshall Plan.) Chilton protested that the Year of Jubilee applied only to ancient Israel (up to A.D. 70 when Israel was crushed by Roman hegemony). He did not see it as relevant to contemporary global economics.

The truth is probably somewhere between these extremes. Neither writer mentions "churning" – that term used by economists to describe the constant ending and beginning of enterprises going on in the marketplace. Most trading volumes are below that surface, relatively secure, but at any given time, some enterprises are winding up and others are starting up. So there are never-ending opportunities for those who have accumulated some wealth and stability to invest into new ventures.

Declaring a Year of Jubilee in South Africa could be worth considering for the following reasons:

- It is a once-in-a lifetime event (every 50 years, roughly our life-expectancy)
- It will not happen just once like a Revolution, it will recur every 50 years
- It is not scrapping Capitalism in favour of Socialism. The market-driven system remains in place and those who lose

land can regain it over time – because that "churning" never stops

- Success is based on performance not on pedigree. Opportunity is opened not closed
- The profit-motive is not undermined, there is simply a kind of economic-earthquake
- Land is released in "home areas" to those who have been dispossessed. So it is decentralized and thus in sync with ethnic realities. It reinforces tradition rather than the risk of expropriating Trusts - which the tribal chiefs are worried about

To sum up, the Year of Jubilee is a kind of Greed Therapy. It shakes those who have become complacent because of their birth or class. It certainly levels the playing field. But it does not "nationalize" all land, or any land for that matter. Land remains privately owned and for those who don't make it, their children and grandchildren are not condemned into an inferior class in perpetuity.

Ultimately, there is a deep spiritual need to control greed. Ancient Israel was a theocracy not a democracy. But the Year of Jubilee model does capture some of the best ingredients of Land Reform that we do need, without losing command of food security, without detrimental policies creeping in, and while averting the worst-case scenarios of economic collapse or worse yet, civil war. God forbid.

The late great Steve Jobs wrote these parting words:

Whichever stage in life we are at right now, with time, we will face the day when the curtain comes down.

Treasure Love for your family, love for your spouse, love for your friends...

Treat yourself well. Cherish others.

Whether we drink a bottle of $300 or $10 wine - the hangover is the same;

Whether the house we live in is 300 or 3000 sq ft - loneliness is the same.

You will realize, your true inner happiness does not come from the material things of this world.

Whether you fly first or economy class, if the plane goes down - you go down with it...

So whether we lose our farm or receive free land from the government, if the economy collapses we will *all* have lost everything.

We are all South Africans. We are all God's children. And God has no grandchildren.

PART 2: POLITICAL PRECEDENTS

1. The Way We Were

Reflections on the 2019 election results

Looking at the map of election results is very telling. They can be found in the Preamble to this book. Here is a thumb-nail sketch:

Year: 1994

Country's population (rounded): 41 million

Number of whites: 6 million (15 percent)

Baseline: Eligible/Registered to vote: 22.6 million (there was no distinction made between eligible and registered because this was the first time that all citizens everywhere could vote.)

Voted: 19.7 million (87 percent voter turn-out)

Attrition: 2.9 million (13 percent of registered voters)

Year: 2014

Country's population (rounded): 54 million

Number of whites: 4.9 million (9 percent)

Eligible to vote: 32 million

Un-registered voters: 7 million (22 percent of Electorate)

Registered to vote: 25 million (78 percent of Electorate)

Voted: 18.6 million (73 percent voter turn-out)

Attrition: 6.4 million voters (27 percent of registered voters)

Year: 2019

Country's population (rounded): 58 million

Number of whites: 4.6 million (8 percent)

Eligible to vote: 37 million

Un-registered voters: 10 million (27 percent of Electorate)

Registered to vote: 27 million (73 percent of Electorate)

Voted: 18 million

Attrition: 9 million voters (33 percent of registered voters)

Trending

Here are some observations on the trending:

1. In absolute terms, the number of whites has dropped from 6 million to 4.6 million.
2. Because of the rise in overall population (from 41 – 57 million), the white segment of the population has dropped even faster as a percentage – from 15 to 8 percent)
3. At the baseline in 1994, there was no meaningful difference between "eligible" and the number who registered. A "stay-way" would not have made any sense.
4. Eligibility and Voter Registration parted ways – with 10 million eligible voters not even registering to vote in 2019
5. As a percentage of the total number of eligible voters, 27 percent did not even register to vote in 2019. That is basically one out of every four citizens.
6. The flip side of this is that the number of registered voters *as a*

percentage is shrinking – down to 73 percent in 2019.

7. This means that at most, 27 million could vote on Election Day. This is the most ever, but relatively few of those are voting for the first time. Most have voted before.

8. However, voter turn-out has also been slipping from the heady days of 1994. It sank to 66 percent of registered voters in 2019, at a consistent rate of shrinkage. Only 18 million citizens cast their votes – *less than in 2014!*

9. Declining voter registration cannot be blamed on whites for the simple reason that its size (10 million) far exceeds the total number of whites in the country (4.6 million). This is very much a black and a youth phenomenon.

In other words, pretty much the same people who decided in 2014 decided again in 2019. They are getting older every time and "it is hard to teach and old dog new tricks". Younger people do not share their optimism in Democracy, so they are opting out.

The people who will be most affected – for the longest period - by decisions are the youngest among us. Yet they are being alienated from the process.

The ANC's inclination to crush its Youth League caused a plethora of splinter parties to appear, starting with the EFF. This kept the old guard in power. Control of succession planning has been totally lost, so the same gang just hangs on to the power.

So those who want to vote for the future – not for the past – are abandoning the ANC.

Perceptions and Misperceptions

The 2019 elections brought some surprises while at the same time following a predictable trajectory.

The first misperception is that only 66 percent of the Electorate voted. This is way *overstated*. The truth is that of the 37 million people eligible to vote, 10 million didn't even register. Then of those 27 million who did register, only 18 million voted. That means that almost 19 million citizens opted out, compared to the 18 million who did vote. By my calculations, that is less than half.

I agree with Luke Jordan, a colleague from the "Commentariat", who calls this a "withdrawal of consent".

When Solon of Athens invented Democracy 2500 years ago, he had just declined the offer of the city-state's citizens to become their new despot. They had always been ruled by the "rich and powerful" but they recognized in Solon a wise judge who would at least be benevolent. Solon's reply was that there was only one way to over-power the rich and powerful – and that was for the Majority to rule. He bet that no minority could hold sway over the Majority, no matter how rich or powerful they were.

His experiment was not hugely successful, and neither was its second incarnation in Rome. To the extent that Julius Caesar crossed the Rubicon with his army and crushed the forces of Democracy. He instituted a family dynasty that adapted despotism into a reign that went on for centuries.

If your perception is that there was just a low voter turnout, think again. Democracy is on the ropes. The Majority has abstained from voting. This is a serious indictment of the status quo.

The second misperception is that the number of small parties in Parliament has increased a lot. It has not. There are now 14 parties with at least one seat in parliament, out of 48 parties that were on the ballot. Compare that to 2014, when there were 26 parties on the ballot, and

13 of them won at least one seat. Only 2 of the 27 newest parties got at least one seat in Parliament. Not much new.

The third popular misperception is that the electoral system is geared to larger parties. In fact, the PR system really favours multiple parties and thus Coalitions. The other system based on "constituencies" or "ridings" tends to favour two major parties. So there is no space for fatalism in these election results. The biggest two parties are shrinking and the smaller parties are on the up and up. This is as it should be, unless government finally listens to the recommendations of the Van Zyl Slabbert Commission's report, and starts tinkering with the electoral system. It recommended a mixed system. A case now before the Constitutional Court may serve as a catalyst to trigger this change?

The fourth misperception is that the DA took a bit hit. In fact, it only lost 1.5 percent over the 2014 elections. That's a lot less than the ANC shrinkage of about 5 percent.

In 2014, the rising star among the parties was the EFF. In 2009 it was COPE. There was talk this time around that possibly GOOD or perhaps the ATM might be the new rising star? In fact, both of them got started, but the real surprise was the rise of the Alt Right – namely of the Freedom Front Plus. It seems that the DA bled some of its previous support to both GOOD and especially to the FF+.

In this is something of a polarization. Because the EFF has showed that it has the magnetic attraction on the Left. Some new parties like the Socialist Workers Party did not even win one seat. Whereas the EFF rose from 25 seats to 44. But the opposite pole to this is that 10 seats from the Alt Right end of the spectrum were won by the FF+. So the ranks of the opposition are in fact growing with every election.

If you categorize the IFP as a Right of centre party, being fairly conservative and traditional in outlook, then the combined IFP and

FF+ come to 24 seats. To a large extent this accounts for the DA's loss of 5 seats. This highlights the DA's internal "identity crisis". Maimane was pushing it gently away from a "liberal democrat" bias to more of a "social democrat" identity. This caused some arch-conservatives to bail out and vote for the FF+ or the IFP. Ultimately, it led to Maimane's resignation, along with Mayor Mashaba and ex-Mayor Trollip.

Likewise, the ANC dropped by 19 seats, and the EFF gained 19 seats. So you can see the polarization of Left versus Right. A lot of socialists within the ANC did not like the way Cyril Ramaphosa articulated some of his business acumen. So they bolted to the EFF.

The fifth misperception is that with a 66 percent majority, the Constitution can be amended to allow for expropriation of land without compensation. There is one school of thought that says this will require 75 percent. The ANC and EFF combined can only muster 274 seats, which comes to 68.5 percent. The hardliners in BLF did not even muster one seat.

Expect to see court action over this question of the correct constitutional threshold. And another worry arises, remembering how Sinn Féin provided cover for the IRA's armed struggle. Gerry Adams was a parliamentary face for a para-military movement. The FF+ will articulate the case against expropriation of land without compensation in Parliament. But this issue could prove to be hugely divisive, and could give rise to that phenomenon of a clandestine insurgency – operating at arm's length but somehow legitimized by the Alt Right in parliament. God forbid, but it would be déjà vu all over again.

A sixth misperception is that only the ANC needs to clean up corruption. Part of the "withdrawal of consensus" mentioned in the first point above could be that other parties like the EFF are also implicated. So it is not just one party but "politics" in general whose reputation has been tarnished.

Seventh and last is the popular misperception that the State President is the boss. The fact is that as soon as the National Assembly elects the President – he must resign as a Member of Parliament. This is a peculiarity borrowed from other sectors where Boards are paramount to chief executives.

South Africa has been brought to its knees by a weak Board with a strong executive branch. This opened the door to State Capture.

Confusing matters even further is that in reality, neither the National Assembly nor even the caucus of the ruling party in parliament really supervises the president. Two Presidents - out of five – have been recalled *by their party*. Non-confidence votes in parliament have never been a real threat because of the cadre deployment of MPs. This harks back to the third misperception above.

The 2019 elections did not elect Cyril Ramaphosa. The ANC won, even though the majority of citizens withheld their consent. The ANC won 57.5 percent of the votes of less than half of the Electorate. That is just over one quarter of the say of 37 million eligible voters. This is rather pathetic and not much to be proud of. So don't be fooled that the President is really in charge.

13. A Laager of Exclusion?

My own concerns about the proportions of those who voted to those who did not were picked up by other "Opinionistas" in the days following the 2019 elections. One of those has already been mentioned – Luke Jordan. Another was Oscar Van Heerden who wrote this on May 15th 2019:

"Are we drawing the wagons into a laager of exclusion?

"Parties with clear race/ethnicity appeal (EFF, FF Plus, IFP) have secured 2.9 million votes. Among these, and often put on either end of a political spectrum, is the EFF (1.8 million) and FF Plus (almost 600,000). These are not, in fact, polar opposites, but the same ideology in different hues, with both sharing intolerance for racial diversity.

"As for the IFP and the FF Plus, these are traditional nationalist parties which cater for members who are narrow tribalists and coalesce around culture, language and traditions at the expense of the rest of society.

"Looking across all the smaller parties — those that are defined by religion and or by race/ethnicity — we see a significant increase in the proportion of South Africans who have given them their support. Whereas in 2014 these parties represented 10% of our counted votes, in 2019 this had risen to 18%. Nearly one in five South Africans who voted, voted for a party that defines itself primarily by identity.

"What we have here seems to be more and stronger laagers forming in the South African electorate. There is a greater polarisation defined by religious and racial/ethnic identity. Much like the laagers of the Great Trek (an encampment formed by a circle of wagons), keeping us inside the circle and them (the others) out, these parties are inward-looking, defining their membership by cultural attributes and not by the battle of ideas. These are the parties that have been growing in the past five years.

These are the early days of Balkanization. But given the right to self-determination that is recognized in international affairs, one or more of these may have put down deeper roots than we would want to believe. For one thing, the Alt Right is now an international movement not unlike the Socialist International. According to media reports, South Africa is receiving regular "coaching" visits from its proponents. Could this explain the sudden rise of the Freedom Front Plus, to a higher altitude, which had been flying at a very low altitude for over a decade? Then it suddenly surged ahead of other small parties in the 2019 elections.

The "Communist Bloc" or Eastern Europe during the Cold War was a vivid example of how various countries can be connected into an ideological network. At times, some countries like Czechoslovakia tried to break out of the common web. Remember the Prague Spring in 1967? It has been echoed in the term "Arab Spring" that has been more recent, closer to home, with popular uprisings trying to shake off authoritarian regimes. Only to find that they were not really free to leave.

One wonders about Venezuela – is it free to find its own way forward? Or is Maduro held by the gravitational pull of Socialism? Will the centrifugal force of Juan Guaido manage to overcome those inward forces? South Africa's alignment with the Socialist bloc on this one puts it out of step with its key trading partners in the North.

Take the issue of land expropriation without compensation as an example. In KwaZulu-Natal province, there are huge tracts of land that belong to the tribal trust. These lands are governed in a time honoured (albeit un-democratic) way by the Zulu royal family. This commitment to traditional practice is enshrined in the state constitution. Traditional leaders are legitimized and included in the overall apparatus of the democratic state. President Ramaphosa has signed off on this.

But if government adopts a one-size-fits-all approach to Land Reform, it will want to reform this land tenure system too, so that individual farmers can hold land title. This is anathema to the tribal trusts. So it is a recipe for conflict.

Then you have the disproportionate amount of land under white ownership. The truth is that accurate statistics on the exact proportions of this imbalance are as scarce as hen's teeth. No one really knows the extent of these disproportions, so they tend to be overstated in the debates, especially during periods of electioneering.

But the general truth is that far more than one-tenth of the wealth and one-tenth of the land belongs to less than one-tenth of the population. This is true in many countries, where this does not align with a racial demography as well. Wealth tends to be concentrated world-wide in the hands of a small fraction of world population. That does not make it right, and is one of the challenges that Capitalism faces where ever you go – how to redress this growing Inequality.

In South Africa, though, Inequality lines up with the racial fault-line that is always there. So it is no longer just a Robin Hood scenario of taking from the rich to give to the poor. It is now a case of re-distributing among black citizens what belongs to white citizens.

In South Africa, more citizens are receiving some kind of direct government aid, than the number of people in the work force. This unsustainable scenario might be corrected if we could just get those millions of unemployed people into the work force.

During the 2019 election campaign, the DA – which rules Western Cape province – claimed that its province has a better record on job creation than any other. Its campaign slogan was to "put a job in every home", meaning at least one self-generated income stream (instead of government aid) into every family dwelling. The tone of this was very different from the Leftist platforms – like expropriation of land without compensation, nationalization of the Reserve Bank, and a minimum wage. Because Leftists think in terms of a planned economy, their solutions are state-centric instead of enterprise-centric.

When you look at the election results in terms of mapping (like map that can be found in the preamble to this book), there seems to be a Great Divide down the centre of the country? It is not geographical, like the peak of a mountain range, with a watershed on either side. It is a mixture of ideological and cultural. My choice of the names for the two zones is metaphorical – Orania and Azania – but it captures an emerging reality...

The forces that divide us are getting stronger than the forces that bond us together.

14. Pan-Africanism Going Forward

Reflections on the conference of the Pan-African Congress held in South Africa in 2014

We named different buildings at C4L after people. For example, one building was named after Charlotte Macheke, the first African women to earn a university degree. Another building on campus was named after Tiyo Soga, the first ordained priest from South Africa – he became a Presbyterian minister in 1856. A Xhosa, he studied in Scotland, married a local lass there, and they came back to South Africa as missionaries in 1857. Needless to say, he was not always accepted by fellow clergy - just as she had challenges adjusting.

Charles Darwin published his <u>On the Origin of Species</u> in 1859. The influence of "social Darwinism" spread fast, being broadly accepted as fact by the 1870s. A fellow missionary of Tiyo Soga's – named John Aitken Chalmers – predicted that Africans were doomed to become extinct. Social Darwinism gave rise to this kind of thinking, like the concept of a super race that drove the Third Reich only a few decades later. Chalmers was upset that Africans were not converting quickly to Christianity, thus his backlash.

Writing in the May 11th 1865 edition of the King William's Town <u>Gazette</u>, Tiyo Soga dismissed the assertion that only a Eurocentric outlook would secure perpetuity for blacks. He pointed to references even in the Bible of blacks and thus to their resilience: "*I find the Negro from the days of the old Assyrians downwards keeping his individuality and distinctiveness amid the wreck of empires, and the revolution of ages. I find him opposed by nation after nation. I find him enslaved – exposed to all the vices and the brandy of the white man. I find him in this condition for many a day – in the West Indian Islands, in Northern and Southern America and in the South American Colonies of Spain and Portugal. I find him exposed to all these disasters and yet living – multiplying and never extinct."*

This heralded the dawn of an awareness that would later be called Pan-Africanism.

The Pan-African Movement

The movement was formalized in London in 1900. An American sociologist attending that indaba was WEB du Bois. His concern at this inaugural meeting was: "The problem of the 20th century is the problem of the colour line, the question as to how far differences of race – which show themselves chiefly in the colour of the skin and the texture of the hair – will hereafter be made the basis of denying to over half the world the right of sharing to their utmost ability the opportunities and privileges of modern civilization."

So the movement began with the intent to secure equal rights for black people where ever they were all over the world.

But in 1915, a Jamaican called Marcus Garvey challenged du Bois. Whereas du Bois was an *assimilationist*, trying to secure equal rights so that blacks could integrate into any setting, Garvey was an *exclusivist*, who believed that different races could not be reconciled. While du Bois championed full civil rights in America for blacks, Garvey promoted a return to the motherland – "Africa for Africans".

One way or the other, the Pan-African movement's focus for its first half century was on the *diaspora*. But that changed with the emergence of independent African states in the aftermath of World War II. Ghana was the first nation to gain its independence and Kwame Nkruma hosted a Pan-African congress – in Africa for the first time – in 1958. Its focus shifted to helping African nations to emerge. This came to pass, and later congresses were held in Tanzania in 1973 and Uganda in 1994 – *and in January 2014 in South Africa.*

In the African setting, these two strategies are not unfamiliar. For example, in the former Portuguese colonies, blacks could become full citizens or "assimilados" if they learned to speak Portuguese, studied the colonial curriculum, dressed in European clothes, etc. The dark shadow cast by this approach was that local culture was of absolutely no value.

Then there was segregation or as it was called in its most Vorwoerdian form – *apartheid*. In this approach, there was space for both – but apart. The "Africa for Africans" slogan took on a more sinister anti-white sense – exacerbating racial tensions. Implicit in this approach is that each and every culture has some value, but some are worth more than others. This has been called "open racism" in comparison to assimilation which is called "closed racism".

Black Consciousness or Black Supremacy?

In assassinating Malcolm X, as elaborated in the chapter called *Where does the African Renaissance end and Black Supremacy begin?*, African-Americans sorted out their own differences without the help of the whites in authority. While this was part of their defiance campaign, the use of such violence emptied black supremacy of authenticity. This was not a case of white supremacists beating up blacks - like the case of Steve Biko. It was self-destruction.

One has to bear in mind that blacks in the *diaspora* are a minority, whereas they are the vast majority in Africa, even in South Africa which still has a significant white population.

- Every time a black is called a "coconut" in South Africa, it illuminates a paranoia that infers that the opposite to white supremacy is black supremacy. It is not.

- Even though there is a huge difference between black supremacy and affirmative action, this can get confused at times; this is often described as *Triumphalism*
- It was inconsistent to be happy that Barack Obama was the most powerful man in the world and yet wish that you could have excluded whites from your own African work place
- Affirmative action in favour of the majority is, in a word, odd
- 150 years after Tiyo Soga married the intrepid Janet, mixed marriages are still very rare in South Africa. Trevor Noah reflects on it in <u>Born a Crime</u>. This primary human relationship should become a future focus of Pan-Africanism. If you cannot get it right at family level, how on earth can you figure it out at work-place level or in the political arena?

15. From Riding Hobby Horses to Riding the Zebra

2008: Reflections on a fading rainbow

The Rainbow Nation has not yet found its pot of social gold. One reason that more South Africans live in poverty today than ever before is its failure to use Diversity positively, as a resource for development. Mandela was admired by whites, while blacks felt that he was too quick to forgive. Mbeki was more inclined to address black bitterness than white fears. He made repeated public pronouncements about racial issues that set off alarm bells. His heir apparent was even more militant. Jacob Zuma's theme song was *Umshini Wam* – Bring Me My Machine Gun. The coup de grace was on Youth Day 2008 when the newly elected leader of the ANC Youth League stated – in the presence of the anointed one – that he would "kill for Zuma". This stridency was indicative of a trend – that the ANC was drifting towards Black Supremacy. Gone were the days of the Truth and Reconciliation approach or even of Black Consciousness. South Africa was on the threshold of Zimbabwesque, proactive, anti-white radicalism.

The foundations of multi-racial, multi-party Democracy were undermined by this trend. For example, a senior judge was investigated for trying to lobby four of the nine Supreme Court judges to be lenient with Jacob Zuma. Just as the ANC bullied the free press, starved civil society organizations of resources, and scuttled the Scorpions, the government tacitly supported Mugabe's cynicism and treachery. For example, by issuing transport permits for munitions to be delivered across South Africa to this Shona warlord after he was out-voted in an election there. Thank God for the combined efforts of church leaders and trade unionists, who acted jointly to block this arms hipment in the port of Durban. Government complicity such as that incident means that it is part of the problem and therefore it can only be part of the solution.

There is only one way to avoid repeating un-democratic Zimbabwe scenarios in South Africa. It is summed up in the same words that God spoke to Elijah when he ran away to the wilderness to escape the wrath of the ruler of his day: *"Turn around, go back down, back the way you came."*

We have to stop riding our hobby horses. Why do we call inter-racial dating "Lover's Chess"? There are other colours in the rainbow, after all. Do we want to live perpetually on a checker-board of black enclaves and white ghettos? To find the path forward, we have to go back to where we lost our way – finding the via media between black bitterness and white fear. That combination is what caused national gridlock in the first place. It has to be revisited and unpacked.

Together, black and white citizens need to meet in frank community-level exchanges that lead to mutual understanding and healing. Otherwise, there will never be much *Riding the Zebra* – slang for inter-racial intimacy. There will only be riding hobby horses – which go nowhere! They will only carry you to one place – polarization.

Community-level forums should not be attended by just one racial group. Buy-in by all groups is mission-critical. The norm is that when the theme of Racism arises, Africans enlist in numbers so that their views can be heard as never before, but whites stay away knowing that there is no excusing *apartheid*. But this becomes a vicious circle. To get out of that vortex, a new tone of inter-action is needed that - without in any way diminishing the pain that people have lived through - will not defeat the very purpose of the exercise. Perhaps the repeated outbreaks of xenophobia in South Africa have made people realize that no race is untainted by the scourge of intolerance?

These forums should be inter-active but facilitated by resource people who are in the know about racism and xenophobia. Open discussion should be supplemented by some structured exercises that are participative and instructive. This acknowledges "the myth of spontaneous development" – that change will happen without facilitation. Not likely – to which current events bear witness. As a French proverb says: "the more things change, the more they remain the same".

A Vision-led way forward

Nkruma said that Africa does not need to look to the right or to the left – it needs to look ahead. A future orientation is missed when people keep looking at the past. For this very reason, community-level forums should be facilitated by youth, whose memory is shorter and who have a bigger stake in Tomorrow. But these youth should not be peddling the ideology of any party.

Cool-headed

When visiting a cemetery in Latvia where countless victims of communist oppression were buried, Pope John Paul II said that while he could forgive, he could not forget. Dwelling on the past and present tends to make people emotional. While deep reconciliation must include the emotions, community-level forums should not deteriorate into shouting matches that people walk away from angrily.

Strengths-based Approach

Too often, change projects begin by focusing on the gaps or negatives. Community-level forums should be positive and look for the strengths that are shared by all citizens. *Build on the things that remain.*

Public/Private Partnership

As stated above, government is part of the problem and thus can only be part of the solution. The ANC has lost the high moral ground that it once stood on, back in the days of John Dube and Albert Luthuli. It now has to share the task of facilitating such community-level forums with actors in civil society. That is not to say that churches and NGOs are entirely without fault, as many such groups reflect the disparities and values that underlie tensions.

Modeled on ProPAZ

In the post-war era in Mozambique, one NGO had significant success in peace-building. It facilitated community-level forums that involved people from both Frelimo and Renamo. This work went on for years and resulted in conflict resolution at the local level, and other outcomes such as the revelation of arms caches. The methodology that ProPAZ used in Mozambique can be adapted for South Africa. If you doubt it, introspect by asking yourself if you are xenophobic and thus typical of one out of four citizens who is, according to research. Repent and reconcile.

Recap

The truth of the matter is that South Africa has not found its way to that pot of social gold at the end of the rainbow. It continues to be fragmented. Blaming this on a third force is just an excuse for inaction. That denialism simply enhances the continental drift that is polarizing us.

What do you want South African communities to look like in the future? When will the time come to forgive - without forgetting? Are there preconditions? Can forgiveness be conditional? Are we ready, as Ghandi put it, to become the change that we want to see in the world?

Every so often we get glimpses that give us hope. Some leaders like Tokyo Sexwale and Mmusi Maimane have been in mixed marriages.

They are finding a way forward past the inflexible way we were – which Trevor Noah's <u>Born a Crime</u> is a grim reminder of. We actually need to re-imagine South Africa and define a new "normal".

The Desmond Tutu Centre for Leadership is ready and willing to start the ball rolling with community-level forums in Mpumalanga province. We welcome the National Forum Against Racism to deploy its youth specialists among us, and to work with and through our Youth Corps members to organize events a la ProPAZ. John Kennedy said that he decided to go to the moon, not because it was easy, but *because* it was hard. It is in that spirit of determination and out of respect for self-determination that C4L is ready to rise to the challenge. After all, its first strategic goal is to promote racial, tribal and denominational reconciliation. *Blessed are the peacemakers, for they shall inherit the earth.*

16. South Africa's Crown of Thorns

Reflections of the Xenophobia outbreaks of 2008

The Chinese write in characters, not letters. Their word for "disaster" brings two other characters together – the ones for "crisis" and "opportunity". There is a lot of wisdom embedded in this.

In 2008, South Africa passed through one of the ugliest moments in its history, one that will be etched in one generation's memory, like Sharpeville was in another's. Whether you buy the government's third force hypothesis; or the critique that international refugees were never handled properly (as part of the quiet diplomacy policy); or the view that Zuma sang *Umshini Wam* a few times too many; or the economic interpretation that the rising cost of living was pinching too tightly; or the Methodist bishop's view that it was all started by the police – everyone agrees with then-President Mbeki's words in a televised address: "*Never since the birth of our democracy have we witnessed such callousness. We must view the events of the past two weeks as an absolute disgrace.*" All agree that the effects were disastrous, even if there is huge variance as to the causes.

This disaster has been labeled "xenophobia" - and with good reason. For it was not perpetrated by one race against another. Mozambicans and Zimbabweans are blacks like most South Africans. Shangans and Shonas may be culturally different from Sothos and Zulus, but this was not a case of racism. It was rather what some call ethnic cleansing. So much for "managing diversity"!

The crown of thorns is a common plant in all of these countries. If these really did compose the crown that Jesus wore through his own moment of anguish and agony, they would have been woven together into a wreath. Xenophobia is but one of several strands in the crown of thorns that South Africa is wearing. Racism is another...

Not long before the xenophobia crisis dominated headlines, there were two other media frenzies – one over black staff being humiliated in a video filmed by white students at the Free State University. The other centred around whites being excluded by blacks at the re-launching of the Forum for Black Journalists. Once again, there was loathing for what whites did to blacks. But the other case was controversial. In spite of the diverse interpretations, there was agreement that it should be scrutinized by SA's Human Rights Commission. Its verdict was telling – re-launching the forum did discriminate against whites. The context had changed from one where apartheid was entrenched in the law of the land, where an FBJ was relevant, to one that is "free and democratic" where an FBJ is redundant. There was some guilt-by-association in this for Jacob Zuma, too, as he had addressed this *imbizo* where whites were snubbed.

When blacks wish that whites would return to their European motherland, it is no different from whites wishing that blacks would go back to their homelands. It is racist and another strand in South Africa's crown of thorns. When Irvin Khoza called a black journalist a "kaffir" it was a racist remark because of the historical use of that term in South Africa. Once again the SAHRC got involved, and demanded an apology from Khoza. Now, every time one black calls another a coconut or an "oreo" (often the default drive when they can't come up with a good argument), is that racism or xenophobia? You can see that there are different thorns woven into this crown on the *prima inter pares* – Africa's economic engine, its leading light, the driving force behind Nepad, and so forth.

<u>Affirmative Action</u>

Another strand is affirmative action. White has become the new black. A Primedia employee was quoted in the press as wondering why white women were excluded from the FBJ *imbizo* because the Constitution "regards white women as black". Changes in gender and even the cherished policy of BEE are both causing huge resentments to well up. The pressure relief valve is emigration. The population of whites in South Africa is therefore shrinking slowly. A brain drain by attrition. One does not see cabinet ministers doing the kind of soul-searching over losses of skills and expertise that it has over the forced return of *'makwerekwere'* to Mozambique and Zimbabwe. But the effects of this on generations yet unborn could prove to be detrimental.

Barack Obama once had to distance himself from his former pastor as it became clear that his own presidential policies and approach were not as radically resentful and insular as the older black leader. He wisely recognized that Malcolm X fell into that trap. He was courageous and looked to the future - not at the past. We need leaders who will publicly declare themselves like he did. When Desmond Tutu critiqued Nelson Mandela, saying that as an influential role model he should not be making state visits around the world with an unmarried escort, Madiba listened. He and Graca Machel therefore married, and kept the moral high ground. Time and again, both Mbeki and Zuma failed to heed prophetic advice from civil society and the media. For example, Mbeki protected people like Selebi and Manto, and Zuma would just not stop singing that militant song when the elders advised him to. He just changed the lyrics.

So if anyone touches the untouchable policy of BEE, they are labeled reactionary, third force, or coconuts! This is yet another strand in South Africa's crown of thorns. Safika founder Vuli Cuba believed that BEE is a disincentive to entrepreneurship. He explained: *"BEE also makes people think that they're better at business than they actually are"*. He prefers the hard work of growing new businesses. Mvela deputy chairman Mikki Xayiya said: *"Since Mvela's inception 10 years ago, it was always Tokyo's and our aim to create a company that wasn't limited to being a black economic empowerment (BEE) company or constrained to investing in SA."*

The last strand in the crown of thorns is immigration policy. So many South African professionals have been "poached" by other countries in this era of globalization, that service delivery in South Africa has slumped. One has to deliberate why this is - in the light of rampant xenophobia, glimpses of racism and run-away affirmative action. The Chinese character for "disaster" suggests that in every "crisis" there is an "opportunity". All of these strands are driving people away – that is the crisis. The opportunity is to reverse that – not blindly, but by welcoming immigrants that will fill the glaring gaps in the work force. This does not mean throwing the gates open at the borders to let any and all in. It means head-hunting the skills that we need to fill the gaps.

South Africa is bleeding from this crown of thorns. Xenophobia is tangled with racism, and that is further complicated by affirmative action that many regard as unjust. Not to mention a self-imposed shortage of skills that could prove to have negative effects as well, unless government relents and allows foreigners to compete for jobs. (If there are any left who would want to live in a country where people necklace their neighbours out of outright discrimination and hatred.)

The crown of thorns was a way of mocking a disputed king. It was also the beginning of a terrible period of torment. But it was a story with a happy ending – resurrection! Hopefully the 2008 levels of self-loathing and introspection in South Africa will just be a low water mark? With God's help, a future is still within our reach in which justice, righteousness and peace prevail.

17. The Pot Calling the Kettle White

2007: Post-Polokwane reflections

Irony or even absurdity is the meaning of the well-known proverb about the pot and the kettle. It is even about hypocrisy – criticising others ·for what you are doing yourself. I have been wondering a lot about some ironies, absurdities and even hypocrisies since Polokwane...

First, there is the issue of "two centres of power". The Zumites said that they wanted to avoid Mbeki getting a third term as ANC president, because he could not run again as state president. So they worried that there would be one centre of power in party headquarters (Luthuli House) and another one in the Union Buildings where the government operates from. Ironically, a two centres of power scenario is exactly what has transpired, for at least another 18 months, now that the Zuma camp has taken over the party leadership, leaving a state president heading a government that claims it has a mandate from a large majority that makes it responsible to all South Africans, not just to one party.

Second, there is the very question of a party being split into two camps. (In fact, it is a congress not a party – often called a tripartite alliance.) The Zumites owe a huge political debt to two of the three allies – the Congress of Trade Unions (COSATU) and the South Africa Communist Party (SACP), for getting into the position of party leadership. Whereas the Mbekites are centrists who do not want to alienate foreign investment. They consider economic performance to be as critical as social issues. In most democracies, different parties put forward their respective platforms – in this case, it is happening between factions within a ruling party! It is very strange indeed.

A third irony is that Mbekites have been complimented for running a good economy over the past decade, when all that was really happening was that they were surfing on a huge wave of global economic boom. As that wave loses its force, cracks are suddenly starting to show in the South African economy. A crisis in the supply of electricity is one good indicator of how well the economy has really been managed for the past decade. This has now been declared a national emergency, and even the mines were shaking, with metals performing poorly on the stock markets.

A fourth point is that there has been some resonance of late between the Mbekites and opposition parties, that represent the 30% who voted against the ANC in the last election. The Mbekites only command 40% of ANC support, which translates to 28% of the 70% of overall national vote won by the ANC. Add that to the opposition's 30% and you have only 58% - not a safe place for the Mbeki government to stay the course. Can Mbeki resist a fair amount of ANC pressure in this position?

A fifth note is that the Zumites have complained for years now that Mbeki has been using state apparatus to contest the leadership race, to punish his enemies and to protect his friends. Starting with Zuma's dismissal as Deputy President, on to the Scorpions investigating Zuma for corruption, concurrent with the protracted protection of a Police Commissioner who has finally been charged with corruption as well. Not to mention the intransigence of refusing to dismiss unsuitable people like Health Minister Manto... when all of a sudden, the Zumites are doing it too! Now that they have ascended to power, Mbekites are fearful of reprisal and wonder if their jobs are secure. Both are cut from the same cloth. The government has been told that it reports to the party! There is even some talk of trying to dismiss the state president before his constitutional term is up. That kind of hypothesizing only comes from a new regime occupying key posts in the machinery of party, parliament and even government, and using this for their own ends. Both camps appear to be digging in for a long war.

So a sixth irony is that all the post-Polokwane rhetoric about unity and reconciliation is a lot of talk but not very much walk. Mbeki did not attend the annual ANC day in January, and the Zumites are talking tough about issues like closing the Scorpions. This one is particularly ironic, in the sense that so many senior ANC figures are currently either charged or under investigation by this special unit attached to the National Prosecuting Authority (NPA). It is hard to escape the conclusion - no matter how much the Zumites might deny it - that there is no connection. Of course there is! In all of Africa, *impunity* is a fact of life in the circles of ruling parties - because these are usually unassailable. Less than ten of over 150 heads of state in post-colonial Africa have stepped down voluntarily. The whole ethos is one that keeps opposition parties, the free press and civil society on a leash. Real or imagined, that is what disbanding the Scorpions symbolizes to so many observers. And this case illuminates the lack of alignment between ANC policy (which as of Polokwane says to incorporate the Scorpions into the police) and government policy (the incumbents created it only a few years ago, when it was hailed as innovative and mission-critical to democracy). It has now come out that a government review of whether multiple security forces can co-exist, or whether they should be unified – which endorsed continuance of the Scorpions – had never been seen by the ANC top brass, those seeking discontinuance. So one wonders how well-informed this policy decision was? This just emphasizes the real reason for it – to create the conditions for *impunity*.

A related (seventh) irony is that the Zumites say that process has been flawed (i.e. overcentralized) under Mbeki whose attitude has been demeaning and whose style has been top-down. Yet their own stances on issues like closing the Scorpions seem more ideological than reflective. Again, they are cut from the same cloth. They are ready to impose their own views rather than listen to other voices in an open society. Even when all opposition parties, representing 30% of the electorate, are adamant that the Scorpions must remain independent. One party even says it may take this matter to the constitutional court. The Scorpions are seen as mission-critical to fighting crime.

This similarity between the two camps within the ANC is also ironic. Zuma has repeatedly stated that there will not be a lurch to the left, and that his policies will continue to go on in the same direction that the ANC has charted all along. So far that seems to be true. The real contention would seem to be about ownership, not substance. A new team wants its turn – and with it, its share of the loot. This is what is so pathetic. When different parties contest elections there are platforms to choose from and voters can decide on which direction they want their country to go in. But when different factions within a party are vying for power, it is not about policies, it is about rewards. The big prize will be to achieve an environment where impunity reigns. So it is ironic that the apparent house-cleaning that took place might be a case of out of the frying pan and into the fire.

A ninth irony is becoming very apparent – soon after Polokwane, Zuma was finally charged by the NPA and is going to court for sure, and conceivably to jail. He is on record as saying that he will resign if that happens. The sad irony here is that the ANC lost all the moral high ground that people like Dube, Luthuli, Sisulu and Mandela won for it. Neither is it a sure thing that Zuma's party deputy will become president in his place. It is also conceivable that he (Motlanthe) will remain the deputy, and that a "by-election" could take place for a new ANC president – to reverse the irony. Names like Sexwale and Ramaphosa come to mind as contenders. This could be a way to get some balance, unity and thus moral fibre back before the 2009 elections get underway.

The tenth irony is the fellow who asked for his day in court, to prove his innocence, is over in Mauritius trying to stop key evidence from reaching his trial. We used to ask why, if communism was such a great thing, they didn't put up a picture window instead of an iron curtain? The same logic applies – if he has nothing to hide, why block evidence from reaching the courts?!

The eleventh irony is the most absurd of all. No substantive change of ANC policy means that party and probably government too will continue to play the race card whenever criticized. Not only has the ANC – in electing Zuma - lost its moral high ground, but for some time now the rainbow nation has not been broadcasting in colour – only in black and white. That is why a white foreigner likes to quote a black South African on a delicate point like this. Xolela Mangcu wrote: "*Over the past few years South Africa's leaders have rubbished Mandela's legacy by their racialization of every little policy disagreement, and ethnic mobilization became a big part of the ANC presidential campaign... Now is the time to reinvigorate the sense of common belonging and creativity that Mandela epitomized... The question is whether or not the ANC has a common sense to recognize how far we have veered from the original promise that our newly created democracy held, and whether the organization will have in it the wisdom and capacity to bring us back from the brink.*" State indifference to the AIDS crisis may have damaged the economy, but this is the factor that has been mismanaged most.

One (black) opposition leader stated that at Polokwane, there was a communist takeover of the ANC! Hyperbole aside, it is true that "run-away BEE" is likely to speed up, not slow down, under the new party leadership – further trashing Mandela's legacy. Power cuts and deteriorating roads are not causes of decline – they are indicators of it. The *causes* include racial alienation, causing the brain drain, and the huge irony of Polokwane is that neither other political parties nor other racial groups are going to feel welcome in the democratic process.

It smacks of Botha offering different parliaments to different races. Any policy that favours one racial group at the expense of others is dangerously ironic. We will end up in a balkanized Zimbabwesque wasteland, not in a pot of gold at the end of the rainbow.

18. Don't call me "Babe X"

<u>2007: Reflections on Malcolm X and the Black Supremacy movement</u>

In Canada, Quebecers have a similar social issue to the Afrikaners and the Zulus in South Africa. They are a French enclave in a country that is otherwise English. Some have struggled for "separation" - the kind of solution that the Nation of Islam had in mind – black separatism. The Quebecers call it "sovereignty association" - not returning to France, but remaining French in Canada. The question that arises in the new century and millennium is this – is there no place left for whites in Africa? Should they form an enclave, or integrate, or leave?

I once thought of adopting the name "Baba X". Baba means "mister" in Zimbabwe. In other parts of Africa it might be "Bwana X", "Babe X" or even "Patrão X". Why the Zimbabwean variation? Because the majority of blacks in that country have done unto others as it was done unto them. They are denying whites the dignity of knowing themselves, of contributing as a distinct culture.

Could this be why the folk ballad *De la Rey* became such a hit in South Africa? Increasing numbers of Afrikaners are rejecting an inheritance of guilt. They are searching for pride in a history that includes repressing others under apartheid but also of being repressed during and after the Anglo-Boer war by British imperialism. Many feel that there is no longer any room for them in the country of their birth. So roughly one million have emigrated since 1994 when the first free and democratic government was elected in South Africa. To those that remain, more than 100,000 copies of the *De la Rey* album were sold.

Boer General Koos de la Rey saw the country's future not in war but in reconciliation. He was more of a Martin Luther King than a Malcolm

96

X, even though he might not have welcomed this comparison! For "reconciliation" to him meant among the white tribes of Europe occupying South Africa, more than racial harmony or integration. But when Justice Minister Charles Nqakula labeled those who complain about the soaring crime rate "unpatriotic moaners", one wonders about the extent to which the current regime is open to collaboration? His solution: "They can continue to whinge until they're blue in the face or they can simply leave this country." This sounds all too much like the ideology of the Nation of Islam that did in Malcolm X, or the anti-white record of Robert Mugabe. You don't have to chase people into the sea to ethnically cleanse Africa, you can do it by policies and attitudes that make them choose to leave. That is what Malcolm X's father taught – that Africans were so unwelcome in America after 400 years, that they should return to Africa.

What is the consequence of either forcing people out or encouraging them to emigrate? It is called "capacity shrinkage". Idi Amin did it when he expelled all the Asians from Uganda. Decades later, the economy is still recovering. Robert Mugabe has done it another way in Zimbabwe, believing that agricultural productivity could be sustained even after dispossessing whites of their farms and redistributing the land to black farmers. The historical record is clear – this has led to economic collapse. Today, Zimbabwe's economy is shrinking faster than any other nation in the world. There is 80 percent unemployment, and a 1700 percent annual inflation rate. These are the outcomes. Black ownership and sovereignty were the outputs. The activities were devising land reform legislation and then subverting it to fast-track the process of evictions.

At activity level, the strategy in South Africa looks familiar. Many see the government's abysmal record on controlling crime and corruption in this light – regardless of the legislation, transfer of ownership is inevitable, so why try to stop the poor from robbing the rich? There is sort of a Robin Hood mentality implicit in this. Most of the all-too-frequent rural attacks and burglaries are initiated by workers with some connection to the target farm. The only other country where rates of violence rival South Africa's is Columbia – where there is an armed conflict. The daily death toll in South Africa often matches that of Iraq. 18,000 South Africans were murdered last year.

The minister responsible for security in Gauteng province was recently robbed at knifepoint while taking a stroll with his wife in the late afternoon near his house. She had just wrapped up a day at her job as the person in charge of public safety in Johannesburg, one of the cities in his province. They did not bother to report the incident to police until there was a huge public outcry. Was it lack of faith? Fatalism? Or just a glimpse of a strategy that is allowing the transfer of wealth to begin?

This has side-effects. For example, 40 per cent of African savings is deposited in banks outside the continent - not at home. So not only is human capital being lost to the Brain Drain – a major blunder in terms of economic mismanagement – but accumulated capital is not being reinvested to create more jobs and opportunities for wealth generation and economic growth.

The UK's Commission for Africa indicated that the number of skilled migrants leaving the continent is pretty close to the number of foreign technical experts being sent in as part of aid programmes. The price tag is described by Professor Alex Nunn of LMU, who has monitored the migration of teachers for the Association of University Teachers: "*A larger home-grown skills base would be beneficial for all sorts of reasons, including lowering dependency on foreign expertise which, as history tells us, does not come value-free.*" There are social costs as well – lost knowledge, history, local ways of thinking, and an over-reliance on externally developed knowledge. Ironically, by driving out the "whingers", these are being replaced by a Trojan horse full of foreign experts.

President Mbeki has connected the topic of crime with the issue of race: *"The fact of the matter is that we still have a significant proportion of people among the white minority, but by no means everybody who is white, that continues to live in fear of the black, and especially African majority... For this section of our population... every reported incident of crime communicates the frightening and expected message that the kaffirs are coming!"* Those whites use every incident of crime, he argued on his weekly on-line letter to the nation, to justify their mistrust of blacks.

Playing the race card is not always helpful. The fact is that – like the above mentioned Cachalia couple, mugged in Joburg after work in February 2007 – the great majority of victims of crime in South Africa are black. They cannot retreat behind razor wire and burglar bars, and their voices are increasingly being heard in the national outcry about crime. Violent as whites had been to Malcolm X's family and movement in the past, it was blacks that assassinated him - just when (and because) he was starting to move in the direction of collaboration and integration. Likewise, ANC politicians do not seem to value constructive criticism, and are too quick to impute racism to those who disagree. Those critics who are not from the white minority are dismissed as "coconuts" - black on the outside but white on the inside.

South Africans of all colours, ages and genders are affected by the lawlessness and lack of security. These are draining away hope and scaring away investment. This analysis is not reactionary, as the ANC would like you to believe. More and more people are waking up to the fact that ANC leaders play the race card in much the same way as the Nation of Islam did – as a smoke screen for their own imperfections.

These include other mistakes that affect blacks more than whites, such as the gross mishandling of the AIDS pandemic – especially the roll-out of ARVs. Not to mention the invasion of Zimbabwean refugees. There are now 3 million of these in South Africa, where unemployment among blacks is a perpetual concern. Are nationals happy that 3 million *makwerekwere* are competing with them for scarce jobs? 1,600 of these are being forcibly repatriated every day.

The legacy of white minority rule is a difficult one. The temptation is to punish your former task masters once you have achieved freedom and democracy. But can a country be called "free and democratic" which marginalizes minorities? While the affirmative action policies of the new South Africa can be understood in the light of its past, there comes a point when this is no more than a culture of patronage. Malcolm X was often asked if the Nation of Islam taught black supremacy, even at a time when it was only small minority. He came to recognize that this over-zealous sort of cultural isolationism becomes counter-productive. Especially when it leads is to a civil service that cannot deliver services efficiently and effectively. Ministries, hospitals and schools struggle to recruit people with adequate skills. Many municipalities can barely manage existing services, to say nothing of expanding the provision of water, sanitation and electricity.

Don't call me "Babe X" because I am a *makwerekwere* myself. I am white but not an Afrikaner. I sympathize with the Afrikaner's search for a new social space where they can reinvent themselves beyond the guilt trip that they have been on for so long. They have a lot to offer South Africa, just as the Rhodesian farmers had to offer Zimbabwe and the Asians had to offer Uganda – especially after its independence. We need integration not isolationism. So often the ugly endings are but a function of leaders who become paranoid and go berserk like Idi Amin and Robert Mugabe.

For so long, the basic distinction in South Africa was between whites and non-whites. Now it seems to be between blacks and non-blacks.

There is a sinister exclusion in this of significant minorities that could either be fully integrated or else contributing enclaves. But blacks who sense this, find themselves isolated, like Malcolm X did as he shed the blinkers of Nation-of-Islam ideology and started moving towards the mainstream of the struggle for social justice. Group-think is overpowering true democratic choice, as it so often has in African elections. The intimidation is subtle but very strong. Debate feels more stifled than it was a decade ago. Democracy as we know it is endangered. Centralization suggests that the government is becoming ever more intolerant.

The rainbow nation needs to manage its "diversity" better, and to make room for *all* its constituents.

1. The Unification of Germany

Watching the Berlin Wall come down in late 1989 was a sheer spectacle. It foreshadowed events in South Africa; it would not be long, we sensed, before Nelson Mandela would be released and the ANC un-banned. For me, watching the Berlin Wall fall apart overnight was second only to watching Nelson and Winnie Mandela walking out of the gates of Victor Verster Prison, holding hands. (With Cyril Ramaphosa on one side and Gwede Mantashe on the other side.)

The end of any war always calls for celebration, but the end of the Cold War was the closure of an era. These two historical events were much more closely linked that one might imagine at first. To unpack this, I will visit two short books, one by Robert Cooper and the other by Sampie Terreblanche.

The Post-Modern State and the World Order

According to Robert Cooper's book by this name, the tearing down of the Berlin Wall in 1989 was more than the end of the Cold War. It also ended a long era during which relations in Europe (and thus the world, which had been colonised to a great extent) were dominated by *balancing power*.

Cooper's thesis goes something like this... Balancing power began after the Thirty Years' War, with the Peace of Westphalia, and trundled along for better or for worse until German unification in 1871 manifested a power too great to be balanced by the others. This brought on the two World Wars – which were really one and the same conflict, with a twenty year armistice in the middle.

As a consequence, America and the Soviet Union were brought into the equation, resulting in another thirty-year conflict. The Cold War is explained by Cooper as a bizarre extension of that conflict: "*the old multilateral balance-of-power in Europe became a bilateral balance of terror worldwide*". Now there were superpowers, as opposed to lesser European powers, and so the colonial empires collapsed.

So in 1989, when the Berlin Wall collapsed - reminiscent of the biblical walls of Jericho - you had not only the end of the Cold War, but the formal end of World War II (especially with the unification of Berlin and Germany). This brought the end of the balance-of-power system, and finally the end of imperialism with Russia releasing the East Bloc, as the Europeans had already done to their former colonies.

Although empires are out of vogue these days, they were the way that the Chinese, the Greeks, and the Romans had brought law, culture and civilisation to many regions. Without these, chaos would have remained. With them, order and learning were brought to conquered areas. However, these were imposed, not invited. The problem with empires is that they bred despots.

Europe's way past the imperialism imposed on it by Rome and later Constantinople was to evolve small states. These were more competitive and innovative, which brought significant benefits to citizens. But they tended to be aggressive. Which led to the need for balancing power.

It was America that pioneered the way beyond nation-states, a trend which is now taking our world in new directions such as the United Nations and the European Union (EU-topia?). America has a way of pioneering new approaches. For example, Bill Clinton's policies and visits to Africa were refreshing. They brought a new twist, in response to African efforts to democratise and liberalise trade. His special envoy to Africa, the Rev. Jesse Jackson, pointed out that the USA now bought more oil from Africa than it did from the Middle East. Political transformation affects economic development, from which flows the improved living standards that Africa is seeking.

Empires, States and Mega-states

Robert Cooper argues that in this new world that we now live in, beyond the Cold War and balancing of power, countries fall into one of three categories:

1. Pre-modern settings of chaos, like Somalia, Yemen, Syria and Afganistan
2. Modern nations, like Brazil, China and India
3. Post-modern federations, like those in America, Canada, and Europe

Countries in the *pre-modern* setting are increasingly marginalised. In some settings, the armed forces simply cannot prevail any longer. Such places are basically *ungovernable*. No one wants to impose authoritarian order in this day and age, so most of the wars in today's world are in these pre-modern settings. There is the occasional external intervention - humanitarian or military - but it is dicey for outsiders to intervene.

The *modern* states behave in a more familiar fashion. Like Saudi Arabia, they don't like anyone else meddling in their internal affairs. The state is sovereign. They like to print their own money, although citizens still may prefer to buy forex on the black market. They are nationalist and can be expansionist at times, as was the case when Iraq tried to annex Kuwait. Worse yet, those people or even tribes holding the power can make life very miserable for other citizens or ethnic groups. For example, when Idi Amin expelled the Asians - sensing that no other (modern) state was likely to interfere. Why else has Africa had such a high level of militarisation for so long, when there have been so few wars across borders, between countries? Military power has been used to consolidate power internally and to crush opposition.

The *post-moderns* have lost their hang-ups about sovereignty. They welcome mutual interference as *transparency*.

Europe has advanced furthest in this respect; the Treaty of Rome is regarded as the launch of this new era, just as the Treaty of Westphalia launched the previous era. Some call it *transnationalism*. All states which participate in it agree to observe, and enforce on one another, stipulated limits and accountability. This breeds trust, whereas nationalism bred suspicion. It allows for disarmament, unlike power balancing which brought us the arms race.

In this new era, there is no *land grab* as territory is no longer so highly prized in the Age of Information. Thus, borders are not a big issue. In Europe there is less pressure on borders than in Africa, because its nation-states originally evolved along the lines of language, unlike Africa, where the borders were often imposed for very different reasons. However, Scots have opted in favor of holding their own parliament - for the first time in almost 300 years. And there is a secessionist party there, that has elected members sitting in the British parliament. Catalonia is looking for an exit from Spain. So devolution is occurring at the same time as regional integration. On this note, the annexation of Crimea by Russia seems to be the exception that proves the rule?

In Africa, where borders were imposed by foreigners at a conference which was not even held on this continent - and with blatant disregard for local language – these trends should be good news. Not that borders should be changed. Just that they can increasingly be ignored, in favor of new and broader systems that unify us. Not borders that divide us against ourselves. A good example that comes to mind is that King Mswati II of eSwatini still appoints tribal chiefs - even in Mpumalanga, the South African province next door. To those locked into the mindset of the modern era, this created a controversy. They saw him as meddling in South Africa's internal affairs. Whereas to those in the more relaxed and realistic post-modern mindset, the tribal and national boundaries (although different) could be reconciled.

Three Problems with Post-Modernism

Problem number one is how to change for the better, without losing what is worth keeping. None of these paradigms is perfect. Nor do most countries fit into just one era. Even the USA is mixed; post-modern in its reluctance to go to war, and yet too powerful to sense any need to yield sovereignty, like a modern.

Certainly in Africa, countries will mix elements of different eras for a long time to come. That is why, while Mandela's freedom heralded a new era, his stepping down at a much later time still marked the end of the previous era. So the first problem is that there is a lot of latitude and cross-over between the eras. The fact is, that "regional integration" is not moving ahead very fast in Africa. We seem to be stuck in the modern category. Ten years ago, there was talk of a regional currency in southern Africa (the Austral?) similar to the West African Franc, a currency used across borders in that region of the continent. But in the meanwhile, some countries like Zimbabwe rather opted to use the US dollar. Finding the road to regional integration is not always easy.

One challenge for Africa will be to grow and integrate in a way that does not destroy its pre-modern elements. Another will be to retain what is best about modern states - their innovation and competitiveness - while allowing the transparency and accountability of the post-modern era to replace what is worst about modern states. For example, ethnic diversity can become a valuable resource, not a divisive factor. Borders can fade, without disappearing. Ancient kingdoms and customs can be recovered, as well as indigenous know-how. Fewer currencies will be a sure sign of progress, just as fewer national airlines could be.

One interesting note is how borders suddenly closed when the novel coronavirus started to circulate in Africa. Even inside South Africa there were voices wanting to limit movement between provinces. Even within the EU, borders closed and planes stopped flying between capitals. So we can benefit from restrictions at times, and from relaxing them at other times.

Second, Cooper wonders whether there are not basically three types of economies inherent in the three eras?

1. Pre-modern: Agricultural
2. Modern: Industrial & mass production
3. Post-modern: Services & information

The concern with this is that countries, provinces or even municipalities could get locked into just one type of economy. A village could become an agricultural ghetto, for example, unable to develop beyond that. On the other hand, it is unlikely that every country will ever produce its own airplanes, or that every town will consume everything that it produces. Just as long as there is room to grow without losing what has been established, this trap can be avoided.

One example is the conversion of domestic water heating to solar power. Most of these devices use "evacuation tubes" – but not one African country yet manufactures this hardware. The tubes have to be imported from China or Germany. So this has slowed down the switch over to Renewable Energy, even though weather-wise, Africa's climate is optimal for solar water heaters.

Third, Cooper warns about *a triumph of the individual in post-modern states* which could lead to such lack of cohesion that it leads to deconstruction - not only of the state but of society. Or at least to its reconfiguration. It is this very concern that causes Cooper's book to be cited in this book about Orania and Azania. Speaking of reconfiguration!

At least one pollster reckons that this is already happening in Canada. It was dubbed a Dominion not a Republic, as it contained more than one nation. But Michael Adams sees a shift to "values tribes" in that society which is well on its way to post-modernity, away from the traditional "solitudes" of the modern era, which were linguistic (French/English) or generational (young/old). "*The movement to post-individualism does not mean a regression to the ethnic tribalism of the past, but rather, a progression to communities of choice based on mutual interest, affinity and need...*" Some call this new age "Heterotopia" and even "Eclecticism". It is a new world which celebrates diversity and pluralism. Is this really a better framework for Africa's ethnic groups to develop their own traditional literatures, economies and home-rule? Or will ethnic ties be replaced by "values tribes", going forward? The following two quotes cast doubt on whether local culture can hang together.

"There is equal need to restore community. Traditional communities no longer have much integrating power. They cannot survive the mobility which knowledge confers on the individual." In his book <u>Post-Capitalist Society</u>, Peter Drucker went on to defend organisations in the social sector as the new clusters in which people find meaning and a sense of belonging.

"This is yet another reason why traditional cultures are dysfunctional in a modern market environment. They rigidly stereotype behaviour with strict moral injunctions, enforced by stiff penalties. These work in closed systems, but they stifle free thought and innovation."

In their book <u>The Great Reckoning</u>, Davidson and Rees-Mogg worried that ethnic groups could deteriorate into ghettoes, the way that the black under-class in America does not *"preserve the coherence and moral structure of traditional African societies. They were cultures of strong families, not cultures of irresponsibility in which 60 per cent of children were born illegitimate, as they were among blacks in the United States in 1990. Traditional African cultures were not cultures of crime, in which 25 per cent or more of the young men were imprisoned as in the modern United States. The murder rate of black men in Africa was not one in thirty murdered by their fellows."* Is this what happens to us when individualism triumphs?

Following the 2019 elections in South Africa, citizens need to reflect on these issues. For example, does the increase in the IFP's contingent in parliament suggest that Zulu nationalism is on the rise? Certainly the rights and interests of tribal chiefs and traditional cultures are entrenched in the state constitution. This has been fulfilled in new legislation signed by President Ramaphosa, although some see it as anachronistic – a genetic throwback to the bantustans. Does this mean that many voters are still thinking in pre-modern terms? How will they engage with a party that not only rules the nation (with eleven official languages) with a shrinking majority, but also takes a leading role in regional affairs (e.g. both SADC and the AU)?

What about the Ba Baroa? Surely they are the most marginalized and vulnerable of all our ethnic groups? Who represents their interests in the corridors of power? Are the rich and powerful not more interested in doing justice to their global responsibilities as a rotating member of the Security Council of the U.N.? Issues like Global Warming are taking precedence.

Last time Donald Trump addressed the United Nations, he told the General Assembly point blank: "I am a patriot". By setting out to "make America great again" is he regressing to modernism? Or is he trying to recover what America always was – not just another nation-state, but the first of its post-modern kind? The prototype.

It gets confusing. Donald Trump in many ways seems to be reincarnating policies that Ronald Reagan would have championed. Yet Reagan was the one who stood at a podium in front of the Berlin Wall, and called out: "Mr. Gorbachev, take down this wall!"

Now here is Donald Trump doing everything he can to build a wall! If this all seems confusing, it's because IT IS.

China once built a wall along its northern frontier. Long after that, it invaded Tibet to the south-west and annexed it. This could have made China more diverse internally (by post-modernizing), but it has rather tried to Sino-cize what was left of Tibet's 6 million people. One quarter of the population was wiped out at China crushed it, and many more fled south towards India, where the Dalai Lama lives today. Along the way are countries like Nepal, Bhutan and Laos that worry whether they will be swallowed up too, by expansionism.

Meanwhile, the Chinese who consolidated in Taiwan have launched another nation, which China says is one of its provinces. Ultimately, if people do have a right to self-determination then both Tibet and Taiwan should have a right to survive. Sadly, China's occupation of Tibet and its top-down policies there are at the verge of annihilating Tibetan culture. And now the Uigurs are being crowded into re-education camps, in China's campaign against religions.

Lost in Transformation

We owe a debt of gratitude to Professor Sampie Terreblanche for writing this book. It internalizes for South Africa how global changes affected our domestic politics. When the tectonic plates shifted, what effect did it have on our country's affairs?

Globally, of course, the 1980s were the years of Ronald Reagan and Maggie Thatcher, who together devised a strategy to bring the Cold War to an end, finally ending WWII, so to speak. The Communist Bloc or "Second World" collapsed (leaving us only the First World and Third World today, or North and South). For a long time there was only one super-power left, which George Bush dubbed a New World Order. Bush was Vice-President under Reagan and just extended that regime by one more term. The rise of China in recent decades is changing that again.

There was no revolution in South Africa after all. Socialism was reigned in. There has been progress, without a doubt, since 1994. It is measurable and verifiable. But it is disproportionate, leaving more discontent than satisfaction, on the whole. That is my reading of the "withdrawal of consent" with only 18 million citizens voting while 19 million chose not to. This spirit of "insurgent citizenship" is reaching dangerous proportions.

Malcolm Ray explained it in these words in a great article in the Sunday Independent: "*It's worth reminding ourselves that democracy, in the ANC's historical perspective, has meant deracialized capitalism*".

That phrase really stuck a chord with me: "deracialized capitalism". Certainly there has been an effort through affirmative action to spread the wealth across the historical fault-line of colour. I am guessing that there are probably as many well-to-do blacks in South Africa now as there are whites. Probably 5 million of each, totaling 10 million. That's a rough guess, but an educated guess. But with a population of 57 million, that means 47 million are still living in the same conditions that people lived in under apartheid. (When there weren't yet even 47 million citizens all tolled!)

According to Terreblanche, it was high levels of consumer debt and government deficits that led to the global economic slow-down that he calls the Great Recession (from 2008). He links this to both bail-outs of companies that were "too large to fail" and to an increase in corruption and corporate criminality. Brought to you by State Capture.

Terreblanche writes: "*The ideologies of neoliberal globalism and market fundamentalism that were sold so triumphantly – and arrogantly – to South Africa by the Americans in the early 1990s now stand thoroughly discredited.*" (p 35, Lost in Transformation).

The jury is still out on whether Mandela sold out the Socialist revolution, but in the context of that era, there was really little else that he could have done. Or else South Africa might have ended up among the remnant of the Communist Bloc with North Korea, Zimbabwe, Cuba and Venezuela. Not exactly the premiere league! Meanwhile we are all wondering if Capitalism is as good as some people make it out to be?

Reagan really existed for one purpose, and that alone. Soon after he took over from Jimmy Carter, the following story was going around Washington... The new President was being briefed by various advisors on different topics. One appointment he had was with the advisor on the Cold War. The advisor arrived and started unpacking his briefcase onto Reagan's desk to brief him on this very complicated topic. Suddenly Reagan leaned across his desk and said, "I have an idea for a policy on the Cold War". His advisor was taken aback, but tried not to show it. "Really, Mr President?" he responded, "What's that?"

Reagan leaned closer to him and lowered his voice: "We win, they lose".

As we watch the resurgence of the Alt Right in America, Latin America, Europe and now South Africa, we cannot take this lightly. It is a force to be reckoned with.

Terreblanche was an academic who made a life-long contribution to studying poverty at grassroots level. He did research and understood the realities on the ground. He did not frequent the corridors of power. But research is always a very valuable tool to both policymakers and development practitioners. Using it, they can make informed decisions about their platforms and projects.

Germany paid a high price for unification. It is no longer divided into East and West. Berlin is booming. Angela Merkel grew up in East Germany, a pastor's daughter. She knows the benefits of unification as well as anyone.

But once Germany was back on its feet economically, she over-reached in terms of her generosity in welcoming immigrants – many of them from Africa. This has cost her dearly, by provoking a sharp response from the Alt Right. Like Donald Trump in the USA, her opponents in both Germany and Europe (not to mention the UK) want to limit this generosity of spirit. The 2019 election results in South Africa suggest that the Alt Right is on the rise here too.

1. Israel and Palestine – the long and winding road

1948 – 2019: A house that is divided against itself cannot stand

I worked on a kibbutz in Israel for a few months during my "gap year" in 1969. Kibbutz Beeri was only about four kilometers from Gaza. It was an area of dry bushveld not unlike much of South Africa. One of the things I did was to help move irrigation equipment around.

This was between the two wars – the Seven Days War in 1967 and the Yom Kippur War in 1974. Israel had expanded and was holding Sinai, the Golan Heights and the East Bank. This served my purposes well, because I was basically in travel mode. I could ride the kibbutz deliver truck far and wide – helping to load and unload cargo in exchange for the ride.

This was twenty-one years after the State of Israel had been re-established for the first time since AD 70. It had started as a fragile nation among Arab states, feeling very vulnerable. All that changed with the Seven Days War – Israel found a growing self-confidence. The kibbutzim had certainly played an important role in establishing the country's economy.

This was my first experience with Socialism, because unlike the country itself, which is capitalist, the kibbutzim are very socialist. They are essentially communes. I came to recognize that where there is a "higher goal" at work in socialism, it can function very well. So I for one do not agree with the cynics who say that Land Reform in South Africa would only lead to a failed state. With my own eyes, I saw the exact opposite to that happen in Israel. It is now 71 years since the State of Israel was re-constituted and it tends to dominate the Middle East. Times have changed.

Israel's borders have been a bit elastic. When it swallowed Sinai for that seven-year period, it more than doubled in size. I think that Sinai is far bigger than the original size of Israel? It was like a python swallowing a goat - whole.

In the fifty years since I was there, the plight of the Palestinians has begun to eclipse public opinion that used to favour Isreal as the "under-dog". Not anymore. Building settlements on the East Bank of the Jordan has drawn condemnation, and only recently has the Trump administration moved the US embassy to Jerusalem and recognized Israel's occupation of the Golan. This can be seen as an Alt Right policy, Benjamin Netanyahu being a leading light on that side of the perennial debate.

The point is that in one lifetime, I have seen maps change many times. Not just the names, but the reconfiguration of borders. History is dynamic. Thus I do not think that the final map of South Africa has been drawn, either. There could end up being an Azania, an Orania, and possibly a Zulu State nested between Lesotho and eSwatini? Who knows? But this happens very slowly and there is pain in the gain.

Turn the SA flag backwards (end to end). Instead of converging two origins into one, its centre-line diverges into two paths. That is what conflict, insurgency, war can bring. The right to self-determination is always there, and some efforts to invoke it do succeed. Not always, though. Biafra, Kurdistan and Chechnya come to mind as ethnic enclaves that did not succeed in secession. It rather looks like Catalonia may not succeed? Western Sahara?

But the map has changed in the fifty years since I worked in Israel during my gap year. There was no Eritrea at that time. Yugoslavia had not yet blasted apart. The Czechs and the Slovaks had not divorced yet. And now Donald Trump is proposing to seal these changes in his new policy for the Middle East. Some are still skeptical, others see it as just a rubber stamp for fait accompli.

This is a cautionary tale. I am warning my readers against something that I don't want to see happen. I have always been and still am in favour of keeping the Rainbow Nation. I worked as an activist in the Front-line States to bring about the end of Apartheid. I have worked inside the "new" South Africa to strengthen civil society organizations. I am neither an ardent supporter of capitalism nor an ardent critic of socialism. I am more of a market-socialist than a welfare-capitalist. I believe that the best policy is to give people a hand up – not a hand-out. For example I would recommend that you read the writings of Henry George over the writings of either Karl Marx or Adam Smith. His book Progress and Poverty outsold all other books in the nineteenth century including Charles Darwin and Karl Marx. His moderate path is the one that I favour.

But in Donald Trump's new map of Israel, I see only gridlock. I feel more or less the same about Netanyahu's on-going re-elections as I do about the ANC's on-going re-elections. These elections are close, but incumbents always holds the advantage. No real surprises in the outcome of either election. And for me, no real hope in either prospect either. More of the same. Corrupt, intransigent self-preservation.

That is why I decided to record my concerns in this book. I see the trending towards Balkanization happening before my eyes in South Africa. I don't know what else to do. I just remember the old Pete Seeger protest song:

I'll hammer out Danger

I'll hammer out a Warnin'

I'll hammer out the Love between my brothers and my sisters

All over this land

Which reaches the right note in the last verse:

It's the hammer of Justice

It's the bell of Freedom

It's the song about the Love between my brothers and my sisters

All over this land

Israel is at the crossroads of Asia, Europe and Africa. It has been invaded countless times from every direction. Yet today it is booming economically and strong militarily.

And yet, at its very gates are its aboriginal people, sequestered, sidelined, even marooned *in their own land*. It is not a song about Justice, Freedom and Love.

I do not want to see that happen to the Beloved Country. It reminds me too much of *apartheid*.

Anti-Semite and Jew

I first read this classic book by Jean-Paul Sartre, one of the French existentialist philosophers, after my time working in Israel. It was my first time to actually study and learn about the topic. In fact, it was required reading in a course that I took at university.

During the Holocaust, sources in Germany like Dietrich Bonhoeffer were reporting to sister churches in Switzerland, England and Sweden (and the USA) what was going on in Nazi Germany. Of course Bonhoeffer was among the founders of the Confessing Church which became the Alt Church, so to speak, when Hitler essentially nationalized the Lutheran Church by appointing a sycophant bishop.

Some people are a bit scandalized that Bonhoeffer joined a network of patriots who planned and implemented an assassination attempt on Adolf Hitler. It almost succeeded, but the Fuhrer somehow survived the bomb explosion. (Although not entirely unscathed.) This only goes to show how strongly people - even esteemed religious leaders - feel about the topic, and the extremes that they will go to, to try to correct the scourge of Racism.

In 1948, the same year as the State of Israel was founded, the World Council of Churches was also established in Geneva. This came less than one year after the "Partition" of India and Pakistan in mid-1947. The WCC went on to establish a *Programme to Combat Racism*.

I was very privileged to get to know the Rev. José Chipenda after his time in Geneva working in that department, and before he later moved from Lobito, Angola to Nairobi, Kenya, as the General Secretary of the All Africa Council of Churches. Chipenda was both very spiritual and a highly intellectual leader. His boss at the time - that is the Chairman of the AACC - was the archbishop emeritus Desmond Tutu. Chipenda played a prominent role in "*A Luta Contra Racismo*". It was a privilege to know him.

My interest in this topic is in part a recognition that ever since the time of Moses and the Book of Esther, the Jews have repeatedly faced the threat of genocide. But they have prevailed. Even though they are still threatened openly by adversaries like Iran.

South Africa will not "solve" its racial tension any time soon. After all, the American Civil War ended about 150 years ago and there are still significant racial tensions there. From Slavery, blacks entered a phase called Convict Leasing. This regress was largely because Lincoln was assassinated – by a white supremacist – just after being re-elected to a second term of office. Then came the Civil Rights movement, punctuated by different variations like Black Supremacy and the Black Panthers. Eventually, an African-American was elected President, who was highly respected (although some of his policies have been reviled and even reversed by the Trump administration).

In South Africa, whenever this topic of Racism goes a bit quiet, Helen Zille tweets again!

Perhaps her most famous tweet said: "Black privilege" is "being able to loot a country and steal hundreds of billions and get re-elected..."

She was replying to an exchange on Twitter involving actor Hlomla Dandala – about white privilege. It is not the first time that Helen Zille has been in the midst of a Twitter furore. This simply serves as a reminder that the topic of Racism is never far below the surface. And that there are very strong opinions on both sides. Orania has its proponents, and so does Azania. So do we want to build a wall to separate them? Or are we prepared to seek "tolerable compromises" that will allow us to live and work together?

1. Hindu and Muslim Partition: India and Pakistan

1948 – 2019: The world's largest Democracy is still going strong

To win a democratic election in 2019, the ruling party resorted to an old trick – sending some fighter jets across the border to bomb Pakistan. There is nothing like firing up nationalism in India to snafu a few extra votes! This rivalry may have grown in the 70+ years since Partition, but it was always there. Which is precisely why the British Raj decided to separate the Hindus from the Muslims in two provinces – Punjab on India's west side and Bengal on its east side - before granting Independence to the two countries. India and Pakistan both gained their independence at midnight on August 14-15, 1947. East Pakistan later seceded from Pakistan (in 1971) and adopted a new name Bangladesh.

This Partition involved the displacement of as many as 12 million people, and some estimates of the death toll due to conflict and plague are as high as 2 million. The scars of this "social earthquake" remain in the cross-border tensions between India and Pakistan up to the present. The Modi government could even be fanning the flames of Hindu nationalism?

One of my personal mentors, the Rev Dennis Clarke, was a conscientious objector during World War II. So he went to live in Afghanistan, one of the few non-aligned countries during the war. He established a business importing and repairing bicycles to support himself as a "tentmaker" missionary. After the war ended, he decided to move back to Colonial India as a missionary. Then came Partition in 1947. He said very little about it to me, but I have heard others tell of his courage during a cholera epidemic that broke out in caring for the sick and burying the dead. It was a time of high drama. Rest in peace, my leader.

The *two-nation theory* at the heart of this decision goes quite far back, to the time of the League of Nations, a precursor to the United Nations. It is very similar to the Two-State Solution that has emerged since then for Israel and Palestine. However, there were and are good arguments on both sides (pro and con).

Essentially, the heart of the matter is: *what is a nation-state?* This is the same question that the Alt Right is raising across Europe in trying to stem the tide of immigration. Their contention is that there needs to be both ethnic and religious contiguity in a nation-state. Two religions that are frequently antagonistic to each other are not a good "fit". Neither are cultures that are intolerant and xenophobic towards one another.

Going back to Robert Cooper's analysis in chapter 18, Europe used the (modern) nation-state model to escape from the (pre-modern) hegemony of Empire. Then along came the (post-modern) network of the EU with its strong bent towards Humanism. If you regard Humanism as a secular religion (as I do), the question of contiguity with Christianity is always there. Europe has been predominantly Christian (in one manifestation or another) for centuries. So when the EU umbrella and countries like Germany (which really conjoins several distinct entities like Bavaria), allow a huge influx of "incompatibles" to immigrate – many of them Muslim - the member nation-states get very nervous.

This incompatibility between Christianity and Humanism goes all the way back to Martin Luther, the great German reformer. And his mentor Erasmus of Holland, one of the early Humanists. Erasmus actually got Luther going, early on, only to end up in an acrimonious academic/religious debate with him later in life.

Thus the rise of the Alt Right and its superstar project - Brexit. Leavers rejected being dictated to by the EU and wanted to regain control over various aspects of their national existence. The looser "network" structure starts to feel too much like Empire striking back! It took so long to shake off Rome's hegemony, that Brussels will not succeed in homogenizing Europe beyond the limits that member states will set. This has become very clear in the rise of the Alt Right in Italy, Hungary, and now Spain. The same centrifugal force that exploded Yugoslavia into several countries is attracting nation-states out of regional integration. Its gravitational pull can only hold them so deep in it, then they find equilibrium or balance.

Over a period of decades in Colonial India, this kind of thinking was debated by indigenous Muslim and Hindu entities - in consultation with the British Raj and the League of Nations. By inclination, some voices were more liberal and others more conservative. The choice of

Partition was not one that everyone agreed with, but neither was it totally opposed. There was a lot of self-determination factored into it.

Opponents of the *two-nation theory* tended to see a future India like the United States model, or the European Union. They were thinking far ahead, in recognition that neither on the Muslim side nor on the Hindu side was there only one ethnicity. There were several. In this regard, it was very much like South Africa, which only emerged 47 years later. We adopted 11 national languages including 9 tribal languages. Afrikaans is also "indigenous" in that it arose first as a creole then later as a written language (thanks to Bible translation). Traditional leaders have been included in the overall governance with elected representatives. (Although sadly the Ba Baroa were missed out on both counts.)

When I see the mapping of the 2019 election results, I really have to ask myself whether this two-nation theory is not where we are headed? Once again, I repeat that I am not prescribing it. I am only describing it. I am worried that "Azania" is more Pan-African with a strong sentiment of Black Supremacy. (At least in theory, while in reality there are regular outbreaks of xenophobia against other African nationals.) While "Orania" is more self-contained and believes as liberal democracies do, in non-racialism. (Again in theory, while whites seem to dominate.) Orania has an eclectic mix of Africans (aboriginal and black), white Europeans and coloureds (whose roots are in Indonesia). Whereas Azania is largely waBantu and proudly African. Would it not be better to build a wall from north to south, zig-zagging down through North-West, Free State and Eastern Cape provinces - and then to "cut the cheese"?

This seems to be the way that things are going. I myself am an opponent of *two-nation theory*, but as I observed in chapter 7, forces like *identity politics* and *implicit bias* seem to be pushing us in this direction. God help us to find one another so that we can find that pot of gold at the foot of the rainbow. Divorces are always costly.

This approach resonates with Donald Trump's effort to stem illegal immigration into the USA. Recent statistics show that even though his wall is only partially built at this stage, the level of illegal immigration is decreasing fast. Illegal immigrants are being deported in droves back to Mexico, and others see the inevitability of getting caught, so they are returning to Mexico on their own steam. There is an element of Partition in this – of the *two-nation theory*. So it is not too far-fetched that this could come to South Africa. Forewarned is forearmed. Read on to know about how it could play out.

Mahatma Gandhi

A central figure in this drama was Mohandas Karamchand Gandhi, who earlier in his life had been one of the founders of the ANC in South Africa. Born and raised in India, he studied Law in London, then returned home. Ghandi was only 19 when he left India at the suggestion of a Brahmin priest, to study Law in London. He was already married and had children, so his family was divided about whether he should go or not. It was decided only after he made a vow before his mother than he would abstain from meat, alcohol and women.

Two years after his return to India, he was recruited by a firm in the Colony of Natal. Remember that there is a large Indian contingent in South Africa's population, especially in Durban. In 2019, two percent of South Africa's population (about 1.1 million citizens) were ethnically and culturally Indian. It was South Africans who first called him "Mahatma" meaning venerable, in the endearing fashion that Nelson Mandela is called "Madiba".

When he arrived in Natal, he thought of himself as a Briton first, and an Indian second. However, the fierce discrimination against Indians that he experienced from whites awakened his spirituality and he became a political activist. At first, this was among his own Indian enclave in South Africa. During the Boer War, he joined an ambulance core, to assist the wounded.

His views broadened after the war, influenced by the pacifist Leo Tolstoy among others. He formulated a doctrine of non-violent defiance against unjust policies and laws. This was a distinctive approach – different from the "armed struggles" that would follow after World War II.

On this note I can once again invoke the name of Henry George, possibly the most influential writer of the previous nineteenth century. His views were championed by Leo Tolstoy, and were compatible with pacifism. Whereas the views of Karl Marx were not, they were relatively violent.

In 1906, the British declared war on the Zulu Kingdom, having defeated the Boers. Gandhi formed another ambulance core – to help the wounded whether British or Zulu. Part of Gandhi's disillusionment with the West was actually rooted in the cruel way that the British treated his stretcher-bearers. He found them to be "uncompromising".

In 1910, Gandhi formed an idealistic community called "Tolstoy farm" near Johannesburg, where he refined his policy of non-violent resistance. In all, he spent 21 years in South Africa, returning to India in 1915 to deploy his political views and ethical principles as an Indian nationalist, theorist and community organizer.

At this point, his personal story merged with the Struggle for Indian Independence that has been outlined earlier in this chapter. That is not the focus of this book.

The sad irony is that this great man of peace died by violent assassination. At the assassin's trial, he stated that he killed Gandhi because of his complacency towards Muslims. In other words, he was a Hindu extremist. He held Gandhi responsible for the frenzy of violence and sufferings during the subcontinent's Partition into Pakistan and India. He accused Gandhi of subjectivism and of acting as if only he had a monopoly of the truth. He was found guilty and executed in 1949.

Just as Abraham Lincoln was assassinated by a white supremacist, Gandhi was assassinated by a Hindu extremist. All because of his mantra of peace and non-violence.

In our time, Asia is experiencing another Partition. Myanmar has expelled the Rohingya. Buddhists are committing a genocide against Muslims. God help us to find one another in South Africa before it is too late. And may we find it through peaceful dialogue, not by armed confrontation.

1. The "Troubles"

1919 – 2019: Reflections on turning back the clock

I am of Irish descent. Which explains my middle name – O'Dowda.

Ireland was the first "overseas" place to be colonized by Britain, so the roots of its settlement there have gone down the deepest. It will be the last place to fully gain its full Independence – if ever.

However, the long-awaited unification of Ireland could still happen. Two relatively recent factors are coming into play. Long after the Republic of Ireland was "freed" in 1921, the European Union was formed and Ireland joined it. This brought unprecedented opportunities and benefits, to the extent that the standard of living in Ireland may have overtaken that of Northern Ireland? Ireland had trundled along for decades as the poorer of the two counties, but now at least they are on a par.

Second, the effect of Brexit is still hard to read, because it is still early days. No one wants to return to a "hard border" between Ireland and Northern Ireland, which is in fact part of the "United Kingdom" of England, Wales, Scotland and Northern Ireland. This was the sticking point that delayed British Parliament from approving Theresa May's proposed divorce agreement with the EU for so long. In the wake of Boris Johnson "getting Brexit done", some pundits think that the unification of Ireland is on the cards? Others think of regress? No one seems to be quite sure how this will pan out.

An armed struggle in Ireland, starting in 1916, led to an Anglo-Irish War starting in 1919 and on to "Home Rule" and Independence in 1920. However, the northern province of Ulster opted out, because it had a higher density of Unionists or loyalists in its demography. So it remained in the U.K. as of 1921, with the Partition of Ireland.

Northern Ireland was predominantly Protestant, remembering that colonization of the island was boosted by Oliver Cromwell, who was a "Non-Conformist". In religious terms, this meant that he was not a Catholic (i.e. "Remainer") or a Reformer (i.e. "Rome-exiteer") but a Radical reformer. It was at this period that the monarchy was suspended for several decades and that the Radicals got the upper hand. Cromwell's conquest of Ireland deepened what its earlier invasions by the Vikings and later the Normans had started. He invaded on behalf of England's Rump Parliament which had defeated the royal army and beheaded the King.

Eventually, Britain got a monarchy back and definitively adopted the "Via Media" or state church that had been launched by Henry VIII and consolidated by his daughter Elizabeth I. Leaving space on either side for the freedom of worship of both Catholics and Non-conformists.

The Republic of Ireland is famously a very Catholic nation. This goes back to its evangelization by St Patrick. The church he founded became the Irish Church during the "dark ages" when the Western Empire of Rome crumbled. The Irish Church went on to re-evangelize parts of Europe like Scotland, the Netherlands and Switzerland. But as the Church of Rome rose up to fill the power vacuum left by Rome's demise, and to become the predominant political force in Western Europe, it re-asserted itself in Britain.

There was a Synod held at Whitby in 664 AD whereby the Irish Church subordinated itself to the primacy of Rome. From this time, the two churches merged and the island thus became Catholic (again) – until Cromwell's effort to colonize it. So over the past century, there has been a political deadlock over the future of Northern Ireland. The Republic wants it back, much like China wants Taiwan back, after all these years.

But Britain has resisted, in the name of the majority of Protestants in Northern Ireland. This gave rise to what the Irish call "the Troubles". This was an insurgency of low intensity guerilla warfare. For 40 years, there was on-going conflict in Northern Ireland. It boiled over at times into bombings in England, as part of the armed struggle of the IRA (Irish Republican Army). Some see this "long war" as a continuation of the Irish War of Independence.

This was finally brought to an end by the Good Friday Agreement in 1998. (It is this agreement that the moderates who negotiated Brexit did not dare to reneg on.) The Easter date is significant because the original Uprising that launched the armed struggle was also at Easter, in 1916. After 82 years of on-and-off conflict, peace broke out.

It is important to note that Northern Ireland had its own Parliament, and the minority of Catholics elected MPs to a party called Sinn Féin. It is this that makes the 2019 elections in South Africa seem like déjà vu all over again. The sudden rise of the Freedom Front Plus within South Africa, together with the rise of the Alt Right in Europe and America, seems to have created the conditions for a similar scenario to begin in South Africa. My worry is that Partition or Balkanization may be on the cards? And my still-to-be-unpacked concern is that this is being brought down on the rainbow nation by Black Supremacy and an over-indulgence in Black Privilege. The game-changer could be the expropriation of land without compensation from white Afrikaners. They are down, but they are not out for the count.

Jerry Adams was the parliamentary leader of Sinn Féin. Of course he had some kind of underground contact with the paramilitary insurgency, the IRA. In fact, his voice and the presence of Sinn Féin in the parliament of Northern Ireland, tried to legitimize to some extent the armed struggle for unification.

Please note that the Irish were always against Partition. But the rich and powerful in this instance preferred to protect Britain's vested interests on the island.

Religion has played a major part in South Africa's history as well. However, instead of dividing us into two camps, we find that both Orania and Azania are very Christianized. This bodes well for the survival of a Rainbow Nation. However, the fault-line that we cannot escape is racial. The way I read it, Orania is trying its best to hang onto non-racialism as a founding doctrine. While Azania is drifting away into self-indulgence that marginalizes whites, coloured, Indians and the Ba Boroa.

Yes, I do understand the history of Apartheid. As an activist, I fought it and no one cheered louder than me when it ended! But again I quote

Nelson Mandela's famous lines from when he spoke at the Treason Trials:

"During my lifetime I have dedicated myself to this struggle of the African people. I have fought against white domination, and I have fought against black domination. I have cherished the ideal of a democratic and free society in which all persons will live together in harmony and with equal opportunities. It is an ideal which I hope to live for. But, my lord, if needs be, it is an ideal for which I am prepared to die."

These should be to us what the Gettyburg Address is to Americans:

"Four score and seven years ago our fathers brought forth on this continent, a new nation, conceived in Liberty, and dedicated to the proposition that all men are created equal.

"Now we are engaged in a great civil war, testing whether that nation, or any nation so conceived and so dedicated, can long endure. We are met on a great battle-field of that war. We have come to dedicate a portion of that field, as a final resting place for those who here gave their lives that that nation might live. It is altogether fitting and proper that we should do this.

"But, in a larger sense, we cannot dedicate—we cannot consecrate—we cannot hallow—this ground. The brave men, living and dead, who struggled here, have consecrated it, far above our poor power to add or detract. The world will little note, nor long remember what we say here, but it can never forget what they did here. It is for us the living, rather, to be dedicated here to the unfinished work which they who fought here have thus far so nobly advanced. It is rather for us to be here dedicated to the great task remaining before us—that from these honored dead we take increased devotion to that cause for which they gave the last full measure of devotion—that we here highly resolve that these dead shall not have

died in vain—that this nation, under God, shall have a new birth of freedom—and that government of the people, by the people, for the people, shall not perish from the earth."

Amen. A great task still remains before us – to build a Rainbow Nation and not to let it fall apart into two or more pieces.

I am of Irish descent. My O'Dowda clan originates from the west coast, near Sligo. I have visited Ireland only twice in my life, once before the Good Friday peace agreement and once after it. On my second visit, I noticed a change – some statues had been erected of my O'Dowda forefathers. They were among the so-called "rebels" before 1998 so they were only celebrated in private. Now they are among the "heroes" so they are celebrated openly.

My point is simple. Times change. Do not assume fatalistically that the way things were when Nelson Mandela was president is the way they are today, or the way they will be in future.

1. "Forty acres and a mule" - a Vision turned into a Lament

1867 – 2019: Reflections on Land Reform

After the American Civil War, many freedmen believed they had a moral right to own the land they had long worked as slaves. They widely expected to legally claim 40 acres (16 ha) of land (a quarter-quarter section) and a mule after the end of the war. The mule would serve for animal traction and transport.

Some land redistribution occurred under military jurisdiction during the war and for a brief period thereafter. But, Federal and state policy during the Reconstruction era emphasized wage labour, not land ownership, for African Americans. Almost all land allocated during the war was restored to its antebellum owners.

Most blacks acquired land through private transactions, with ownership peaking at 15,000,000 acres (6,100,000 ha) in 1910. Most of that land was in 4 states - Alabama, Mississippi, North Carolina, and South Carolina. This figure has since declined to 5,500,000 acres in 1980 and to 2,000,000 acres in 1997. Most of this land is not the area held by Black families in 1910; beyond the "Black Belt", it is located in Texas, Oklahoma, and California. The total number of Black farmers has decreased from 925,708 in 1920 to 18,000 in 1997; the number of White farmers has also decreased, but much more slowly.

Black American land ownership has diminished more than that of any other ethnic group, while White land ownership has increased. Black families who inherit land across generations without obtaining an explicit title (often resulting in tenancy in common by multiple descendants) may have difficulty gaining government benefits and risk losing their land completely. Outright fraud and lynching have also been used to strip Black people of their land. Government policies – especially in the USDA - have not been conducive on the whole to keeping African Americans on the land.

So the phrase "40 acres and a mule" has come to symbolize the broken promise that Reconstruction policies would offer economic justice for African Americans. It even took a decade or so, after the American Civil War, for the freedmen to become citizens.

Zimbabwe – déjà vu all over again

Since Emmerson Mnangagwa replaced the late Robert Mugabe as President of Zimambwe, he has been trying to convince white farmers to return, and to find a way to reverse the expropriation of their farms. But there is a lot of skepticism among the farmers who were evicted.

Even though Mnangagwa is only echoing many black voices among the unemployed and impoverished there, pining for their return.

Food security in Zimbabwe took a tumble in more recent years, after the initial phase of land reform under the Lancaster Agreement proved to be too slow. It had proceeded cautiously at first, during that period of transition, because of the lessons learned in America after the Civil War. But it was speeded up to the extent that implementation parted ways from policy. Some feel that the policy was good, but that "triumphalism" overtook it and that's when it got messy.

Things do not always turn out as you want them to. Since the EFF and ANC voted 241-to-83 to form a committee to explore if and how to amend the "never-again constitution", debate in the media has generated more heat than light. But some points are worth noting:

- **Mondi Makhanya** – But what are they doing in the cities if they are land-hungry? Well, that is the whole point. They are seeking a place in the modern economy, having fled the basic-ness of a peasant existence. In many cases, they have left arable land behind in the countryside, driven by the belief that life in urban areas offers social mobility for them and their children... what we are now doing as a country is making "the return of the land" an article of faith – so much so that we are even prepared to break the Constitution to achieve what implementation of policy can achieve. We are prepared to lie to "our people" and tell them that the "return of the land" is the great panacea.
- **Jesse Duarte** - The Land Audit Report: Phase 2, which deals with the scope of privately owned land, released in November 2017, highlights that White South Africans continue to own 72 percent of private owned land in South Africa. This is followed by Coloureds at 15 percent, Indians at 5 percent and

Africans at 4 percent. In other words, Whites own more than eighteen times the amount of land than Africans do.

- **Roelf Meyer** - ITI's research division shows government owns 4 323 farming units, which include smallholdings and bigger farms. This land was bought following successful land claims against these properties. However, the farms have never been transferred to their new owners... it doesn't make sense to expropriate more farms if government does not have the capacity to transfer the farms already bought to future farmers.

- **Enoch Godongwana** - "We are saying people who are landless but who work the land must own it. It also applies to the West Rand, for example: you have got 124 mineworkers who own a herd of 4 700 cattle and they don't have grazing lands. In rural areas people are working the land but don't have any land."

- **Anthea Jeffrey** - Of the roughly 76,000 successful claims in post-apartheid South Africa's restitution process, begun in 1994, only about 5,800 chose to have land returned to them. The remaining 92% preferred cash compensation instead. Comprehensive opinion polls commissioned by the SA Institute of Race Relations (IRR) have repeatedly shown that most black South Africans have little interest in land reform. The IRR's 2017 field survey, only 1% of black respondents identified "speeding up land reform" as a top priority for the government.

- **Ngwenya-Mabila** - argued in the parliamentary debate that expropriation must be subject to just and equitable compensation as indicated in section 25(2)(b) of the Constitution, the amount of which and the time and manner of payment of which must have been agreed to by those affected or decided or approved by a court.

- **Jeremy Cronin** – says that the Constitution as it stands is adequate to expropriate land. There is no need to amend it to do so.
- **Nelson Mandela** - "we knew land reform would not be an easy task or quickly achieved. In other countries it has taken decades, even centuries, and it is still not complete..."

Beware Venezuelan socialist rhetoric

In recent years we have seen Socialist rhetoric being used as mere "fronting" for State Capture. The epitome of this has been in Venezuela. Ironically, Malema of the EFF championed Chavez as a great leader, and this is cause for concern. Chavez was a bank robber who didn't wear a bandana, instead he memorized and spouted Socialist jargon, while looting his nation's petrodollars on an unprecedented scale.

Today there is no food security, and a great deal of hunger. It is worse even than Zimbabwe. There are worries of total economic collapse. Beware populists who are not even on a land grab – they are on a power grab.

Finding one another

The fact that there are practicing Christians on both sides of this dispute is an opportunity to find convergence and use it to build a Solution. This can provide a historic road-map to ending poverty by reducing the glaring disparity between rich and poor. Where God is in charge, such a huge gap is unacceptable.

There are three distinct views. First, that land is "private property". This was espoused by Adam Smith. Second that all land belongs to the State. This was Marx's view. The third view has a far longer history, but has been out of vogue in recent centuries. That is, that the land belongs to

God. There may be more to the Jubilee principle than most voices are willing to concede.

For example, an American prophet called Henry George presented a "third way" late in the nineteenth century. He had a huge influence on people including Franklin Roosevelt, as he looked for coping strategies during the Great Depression. How can you assist the poor and unemployed without undermining economic growth? This "via media" has taken on diverse manifestations during the past century. South Africa would do well to look for such a moderate way forward. Land reform? Yes. Expropriation without compensation? No. One key element in the thinking of Henry George is that the benefit of land and natural resources must be shared by all. They cannot be privately owned, and that is very close to the notion of Jubilee. He believed that farmers should benefit from the return on their investments of inputs and labour. But they should always have to pay for land and natural resources (like water) because these cannot be sequestered by private ownership. There are mechanisms to do this. There is also room for innovation and creativity.

The problem is, there is no Panacea

A short digression is needed here. In the early years of the bloody American Civil War, it did not go well for the Union (i.e. the North). Casualties were terribly high, thinning out the numbers of fighters. That is, until President Abraham Lincoln started recruiting black troops. This shored up his number of soldiers – a key factor in winning the war. So they naturally had a feeling of entitlement when it was all over.

In South Africa, urbanization and industrialization was predicated on cheap labour from those who were displaced from rural areas. The extent to which this was forced by "dispossession of land" or simply the trending of that time is debatable. COPE leader Lekota disagrees that most land was "stolen", and has joined forces with Afriforum to espouse a different narrative – without denying the obvious need to speed up land reform. This imperative is not disputed.

However, there is a strong sense among black citizens that South Africa's level of development could never have been achieved without their input – even under *apartheid*. So they are not only stakeholders, but their high expectations are based on what is sometimes called "sweat equity". This also explains their sense of entitlement to take back possession of land.

In America - over the past century - while the colour of land ownership has shifted in favour of white farmers, another fact is also true in the USA. Because of mechanization of farming, the overall population of the rural areas has declined. More people – even and especially whites – have moved to towns and cities. But this same shrinkage occurred faster among black farmers than among white farmers.

This makes me wonder about a sudden "back to the land movement" emerging in South Africa. Is the "expropriation without compensation" debate really about an inclination to take up farming? If so, why then are only 3 percent of post-secondary students enrolled in Agricultural courses – Africa-wide?

The document recently "leaked" from the Thabo Mbeki Foundation is spot on. It warns against any land reform strategy that destabilizes the equilibrium of non-racialism. It warns that the ANC could be moving in the direction of the PAC, which parted ways long ago because the historic ANC always championed non-racialism.

Certainly the language of the great debate about land reform has generated more heat than light about this "back to the land movement". That is why the example of that erstwhile dream of "forty acres and a mule" is so relevant. It contained more of a sense of entitlement than a sustainable economic strategy.

South Africa is such a diverse country in geographical terms – Lowveld and high plateau, desert and dense forest, temperate high altitude and hot humid sea level, rich loam and sandy gravel, near to city markets and far from urban areas - that it would be hard to define a Panacea like "forty acres and a mule". The rallying cries in the run-up to the 2019 election are "expropriation without compensation" and "radical economic transformation". These are now being answered by the DA's slogan: *One South Africa for All.*

There seems to be a consensus that land reform in South Africa is an imperative. No one denies that. But there are still two related issues – the rule of law and keeping non-racialism intact. Any approach that illegally occupies land or that incites violence is unwelcome. There is adequate land for everyone, and a new recognition of the urgency of a Year of Jubilee. Both blacks and whites are citizens, and most of them are people of deep faith. In the spirit of Jubilee, citizens who have become marginalized need to be brought back into the mainstream again. Those who are economically dependent of social assistance need to become economically active again. This is not just their problem, it is everyone's problem. Those who are prospering are corporately responsible to make space and create the conditions for this to happen. And a democratically elected government is the best arbiter you can ever find, anywhere.

However, if party platforms or government is expecting to find a one-size-fits-all Panacea, history will repeat itself and this new "back-to-the-land movement" will fail like the vision of "forty acres and a mule" during the post-war Reconstruction period in America. Any party that over-simplifies the complexity of this problem and therefore of its solution, is not worth electing. You cannot just say "They stole the land" or "If the white farmers leave, food security will leave with them". That is just electioneering. Politicians only think of the next election; statesmen think of the next generation.

1. Déjà vu from the Life of Lincoln

1865: Reflections on unexpected conflict

In his whole life, he spent less than a year in a classroom. He grew up on the frontier, moving from one rural setting to another as his father tried to find better land to farm. The law obliged him to work for his father until he was 21 – even though his Dad was abusive. He left home the day he turned 21 and years later refused to attend his own father's funeral. It was a strong statement. Some people interpret his unusual empathy with African slaves as deriving from his father's abuse and exploitation of him.

Abraham Lincoln taught himself how to read and write and he borrowed books whenever he could. After he left home, he wandered. He urbanized, he worked in different jobs. He kept studying and after three years he obtained his license to practice law. He was ambitious and determined to overcome the disadvantages he had grown up with. He joined a law firm and started a family, in Springfield, the state capital of Illinois.

I have to admit that this narrative resonates a bit with the upbringing of Nelson Mandela. The difference being that Abraham Lincoln, arguably America's greatest president, was not born into a royal family with any privileges at tribal level. Lincoln was the quintessential self-made man.

During a war with a local Indian tribe, he enlisted in the militia. His troop of men chose him to be their leader, an honour which he later said meant more to him than any other. Suddenly he had a taste of leadership and those militia skirmishes would be his only military exposure prior to taking on the mantle of Commander in Chief at the outset of the bloody American Civil War.

He dabbled in local politics, gaining some experience in debate and public speaking. His first great policy challenge was to debate that Democracy was incompatible with Slavery. This was because some of the new territories to the west of Illinois were debating whether to legalize Slavery or not. He served two terms in the provincial legislature and one term in Washington, as a legislator, for the Whig party.

When he ran for the Illinois seat in the Senate, but lost. It looked like the end of his political career; like he would have to be content with his law career.

But two years later, he managed to win the nomination to run for president under the newly formed Republican party. He won on the third round, as a compromise candidate, in Chicago.

He was physically awkward, ugly and so rural that he was considered too informal. Even after he moved into the White House, he would receive people at times in his bare feet. But he was so affable and honest that ordinary people could relate to him.

His first presidential race was against three other candidates. Fortunately for him, they split the vote, to the extent that he won - even though he had only garnered 39 percent of the votes. This election was virtually a referendum on the expansion of Slavery into the new states in the West. His victory stopped that. But it riled up the southern states, whose economy was based on Slavery.

In South Africa, the 2019 election was a kind of referendum on another question - land expropriation without compensation. The debate raged about that policy issue, just as the expansion of Slavery issue was a raging debate in the years before Lincoln was elected.

His analysis was that Democracy was unfairly contrived because representation in Washington was disproportionate. This is because slaves were counted at three-fifths of a person (60 percent human) which gave the southern states an edge in the vote-counts, that in turn perpetuated the status quo. As a lawyer and a politician, Lincoln took exception to this, much like the citizens of South Africa objected to the structural injustices of colonialism and apartheid, and to contrivances like a tricameral Parliament.

In those days it was a two-week train trip to travel from Illinois to Washington. While making his way to Washington, for his inauguration, Lincoln learned that one state had seceded from the Union. Others followed, and soon they joined in a Confederacy. To Lincoln, this was illegal and treacherous, as the Union had even preceded the Constitution.

South Africa needs to think through the "repercussions" of what will happen if land is expropriated without compensation, particularly if the Constitution is changed to streamline that. For there could be knock-on effects - on the banks, on foreign investment, on race relations, and so forth. At the root of this is the notion of private property, which to some citizens is sacrosanct. That is not my personal belief, for I believe that the land belongs to God. I therefore endorse proactive land reform, but always in the context of the rule of law, and in a way that bonds different races together - not one that shakes non-racialism. There are such strategies, though some regard these as too "moderate" and not "radical" enough.

One can see an evolution in Lincoln's thinking over time. The American Civil War began as an attempt to keep the Union intact, preventing any states from seceding – an act of treason. In fact, Slavery was still legal in four states of the Union which Lincoln could not dare to lose. But in the early years of the war, it went badly for the North.

They started with superior troop numbers, but these were depleted by very heavy casualties. Then Lincoln took a step that was not even considered at the beginning of the Civil War. He started to enlist black troops. He racially-integrated the army.

This inspired him to return to his arguments against the expansion of Slavery into new states in the West. That had not made him an "Abolitionist" back then, when he had been prepared just to contain it in the states where it already existed. But when he composed the Emancipation Declaration in the middle of the Civil War, it was a game-changer. He moved the goalposts from keeping the Union intact, to liberating slaves. This position was controversial even in the North. In fact, it was a white supremacist in the North who assassinated Lincoln, soon after the war was won.

Meanwhile, Lincoln managed to pass the Thirteenth Amendment, freeing the slaves. He managed to win the war after four years of bloodshed on a scale never seen before. And he managed to win a second presidential election. Only to be assassinated soon thereafter.

Looking back, Lincoln was elected with very little education and almost no experience in the executive branch of government. Nor did he have any military experience to speak of. Yet he led the Union to victory on the battlefield, thereby keeping the Union intact. The post-modern experiment in America got a new lease on life. On the way, he freed the slaves, a moral and social victory on top of his military and political successes. And he was only 56 years old when he was assassinated by an extremist.

South Africa seems to want to elect leaders who are already in their sixties or seventies, even though life expectancy here is only 50 years for men. So many competent young cadres are being overlooked. It seems almost silly for Zimbabwe to elect a 75-year-old to start a new era.

Lincoln was thrifty and honest. These are not virtues that come to mind in South Africa, where leaders have two distinct vices – waste and corruption. Waste is not illegal, it is just immoral in a country with so much poverty. Corruption is illegal, and is a cancer that weakens the country's economy and morale.

Above all, if Land Reform is an imperative – and I believe that it is – why can't it evolve slowly like Lincoln's thinking? Why do we suddenly need to amend the Constitution? Certainly the Abolition movement was active, but Lincoln himself was no radical. He was a lawyer, a politician and ultimately a statesman. This takes patience and moves with glacial slowness at times. Slowly but surely. Sequentially. Cautiously.

"When you want to go fast, go alone. When you want to go far, go together."

PART 3: UP CLOSE AND PERSONAL

25. Where does the African Renaissance end and Black Supremacy begin?

THE opposite of white supremacy is not black supremacy - it is social cohesion. The opposite of ethnic cleansing is not just co-habitation – it is non-racialism. The opposite of self-segregation is not forced integration – it is reconciliation and collaboration.

Fragmentation and alienation can lead to conflict and chaos, to which occasional blow-outs in Kenya bear witness. Instead of perpetual bitterness born of centuries of oppression, the best of African hospitality could show kindness to the strangers in our land. Instead of an inferiority complex born of mind games, the best strategy in an age of globalization that bridges continents is cross-racial coalition. Instead of messiah complexes that manifest themselves in arrogance and impunity, the way forward is through new attitudes of tolerance, respect and inclusion.

Achille Mbembe wrote: *"For black solidarity to remain the moral struggle it used to be, it must be rooted in a commitment to equal justice for all, blacks and whites. A conception of blackness that isn't concerned with promoting non-racialism is anachronistic. The goal of black solidarity and black economic assertion should always be to deepen South Africa's democracy."*

The "two-nation theory" examined in Part 2 of this book uses the litmus test of whether two religions or two ethnicities are "frequently antagonistic". Yet Partition causes an earthquake as populations are displaced to de-homogenize them. Instead of milk, you get curds and whey. But then people can settle down to a life without daily stress and anxiety caused by unrelenting conflict with their neighbours. Surely this is the scenario that the Alt Right in Europe is trying to avoid –

not letting too many "incompatibles" cross the Mediterranean. Donald Trump is building a wall...

So why are cracks appearing in the pillars of democracy?

- **Good governance** - the ruling party has made an open effort to assert itself over the government. The state president, they say, reports to the party president. So the party can command the government to close an elite police unit that many citizens and opposition parties see as mission-critical to fighting crime. Who is in charge, really? Do we live in a constitutional democracy where Parliamentary oversight rules? Or in a Soviet Socialist Republic where a Vanguard party rules?
- **Separation of powers** – Not only is parliament made redundant by the ruling party's command structures, but interference in the Judiciary has been a huge concern. Party officials have openly intimidated judges who they thought would not dare to convict their leaders. Just as Parliament needs to be recomposed to diminish the phenomenon of cadre deployment, so also the independence of the Judiciary and Section 9 institutions must be protected. One way is for the appointment at senior levels to be transparent.
- **Rule of law** - When a state president or a provincial premier is not above manipulating law enforcement, the party will be perceived to be standing behind his threats. Not only did the ruling alliance elect a party president who many regarded as unfit for office, but when the party tried to correct its mistake, numerous others with dubious track records still rank high in the party. They call that "unity". Impunity still reigns. Unless and until citizens can see some convictions, sentencing and recovery of stolen wealth, few will trust the ruling party again. This explains the Electorate's "withdrawal of consent".
- **Loyal opposition** – The huge majority once held by the

ruling party is shrinking, slowly but surely. However, this has never stopped it from bullying opposition parties and their leaders. Most curious of all is the emergence of two factions inside the ruling alliance, one of which is effectively serving as the stabilizer, the other as the destabilizer. Will we end up with a "hung parliament" like Theresa May did? Because our ruling party is really two factions.

- **Human rights** – There too few non-blacks in the upper echelons of the ruling party's leadership. The white population of South Africa dropped from 6 million to 4.9 million in the first decade after the dawn of democracy. It is expected to keep dropping (drooping?) by about 1 million per decade. These people are leaving for a reason; they see no future in a country that has moved beyond non-racialism towards Black Supremacy.

- **Freedom of expression** – Government officials are always terrified of a "purge" following the change of party leadership. Unions have been split over loyalty issues, weakening the labour movement. One could even speak of the balkanization of organized labour. Only some unions are now part of the ruling alliance, others are on the outside. Independent media voices and non-state actors have held their own and are keeping democracy alive. They may be is less danger now that before the New Dawn? But this is hard to read because one of the two factions inside the ruling party is still hazardous to the health of newswomen and men. Just ask Ferial Haffajee!

- **Inclusive economy** - Although it has not got to the point of expelling the merchant class for racial reasons as Idi Amin did to the Asians, affirmative action is going over the top. Some call EconoBEE by another name – "Ought-not-to-BEE"! This policy is seen by many as benefiting only an elite, while hurting the overall economy.

- **People-centred** – "Batho Pele" is a bit ironic in the light of the degradation of public service delivery. The standards in hospitals and schools have been eroding. Crime and corruption were out of control and did untold harm to the SOEs. Eskom in particular is failing to deliver *power to the people* – because all it thought about for decades was the demand side, not the supply side. The mad dash to Nuclear had to be stopped by a small nonprofit organization taking the government to court.

Clem Sunter, a leadership analyst, wrote: "The country is now in the relegation zone and faces possible ejection into the economic mire of the second division. And this could happen quicker than we think." Not only sports fans will mind if South Africa slips from the big leagues to the minor leagues! The Rand has already started to slide... in this, the Eskom debacle looms large.

Mondli Mkhanya, editor of the Sunday Times, wrote: "We are watching the dream slip through our fingers, and there seems to be no sense of urgency among our leaders about rescuing it."

Malcolm X

Malcolm X is an African American folk hero. He is to America what Steve Biko is to Africa – the premiere voice of black consciousness. Like Biko, his views were penetrating. They had some roots in the teachings of his father, who believed that black Americans should all migrate back to Africa, being unwelcome in America even a century after its civil war. The influence of Elijah Mohamed shaped his views, until his own discerning insights began to see through even the charades of the Nation of Islam, that had brought him from prison to the status of national spokesman for Black Supremacy. This group taught that blacks should first and foremost come to terms with their own identity and shake off the colonization of the mind that kept them enslaved to white agendas - long after slavery was abolished. It refused to cooperate with whites, or even with other civil rights groups that promoted integration with whites. It was fiercely proud of its heritage and constituency: black is beautiful.

As Malcolm X began to perceive the Nation of Islam's imperfections, he began to open up to collaboration with other civil rights groups. This was anathema to his long-time sponsors. Seeing it as betrayal, they assassinated him. Thus, African Americans sorted out their own differences without the help of the whites in authority. While this was part of their defiant isolationism, the use of violence emptied it of authenticity. It was not a case of white supremacists beating up blacks - like Steve Biko. Is blacks-murdering-other-blacks better or worse? Does it validate Black Supremacy? We have to ask this question every time there is another political murder in South Africa.

This case study is instructive, but one has to bear in mind that blacks are a one-in-ten minority in America, about the same as whites are now in South Africa. Every time a black is called a "coconut" in South Africa, another nail is driven into non-racialism's coffin. There is too much of that paranoia that concludes that the opposite to white supremacy is black supremacy. It is not.

Abraham Lincoln was also assassinated – soon after he won the civil war, to free the slaves. But he was white, as were so many of the abolitionists. Obviously, the blacks had previously been slaves in America, not the colonial oppressors that the whites have been in the African context. So it took a lot of white influence – coupled with black activism – to end slavery. But still there is a parallel – South Africa needs new leaders with the insights of Malcolm X and Steve Biko and with the courage of Abraham Lincoln and FW de Klerk. Remember that Nelson Mandela was still in prison when de Klerk took over with a mandate for change. It will take more than whites continuing to engage the powers in the new South Africa to rescue the rainbow project. It will take black leaders who recognize the importance of not driving non-blacks away. Nelson Mandela clearly did, but Mbeki and Zuma have both failed in this respect. They lost the moral high ground...

Achille Mbembe wrote: *"Thanks in a large part to the Truth and Reconciliation Commission, the world came to believe that South Africa offered an ethical alternative to the violence of the present. It saw in the South African experiment the sign of an even more radical Utopia, that of a world without racism. Today, the country is facing a fragile, confusing and uncertain present. The dramatic moral failure of our political leadership is now evident."*

This ethical failure is reflected in:

- Immorality
- Eroded work ethic
- Attitude of entitlement
- Acquiescence to mediocrity
- Complacency
- Arrogance
- Low sense of social responsibility

The conditions that are manifested by this breakdown include:

- Crime
- Corruption
- Government intransigence
- Manipulation of state organs
- Impunity
- Intimidation
- The race card

- Deteriorating services (e.g. electricity crisis)

One wonders if the ruling alliance is simply not too diverse and too over-representative to function in the context of pluralism? What is a party that operates like a one-party state doing in a multi-party Democracy any way? This pride is causing it to dis-integrate. In humility, it would be smaller but more sustainable.

It is certainly big enough to try its hand at controlling and/or intimidating the media, not to mention law enforcement agencies and even the judiciary. So big that it is also inclined to keep civil society on a leash, by centralizing the flow of resources. And by covert surveillance of private voluntary organizations. In most countries, trade unions are part of the composition of this "third sector", but in South Africa they have been part of the ruling congress. This has a detrimental effect on the role of the civil society - conveniently for government. A number of trade unions have now recognized this and marched out of the ruling alliance into civil society, weakening its unity but restoring some authenticity to it.

Is not the conspicuous lack of inspiring leadership related to the fact that the ruling alliance is simply too big to stand for something anymore? It stands for *everything* instead. And thus for nothing. Could that explain, deeply, the leadership vacuum? Or the "withdrawal of consent" by a majority of the Electorate who did not even bother to register and/or vote in 2019?

In this final section of the book, I am taking some huge personal risks. I want to capture the look and feel of this prevailing attitude of Black Supremacy *at ground level*. In doing so, though, I have to be very careful and very selective. I do not mention any names, so that the message is genericized. Many details are left out, to simplify the storyline so that it is accessible and relevant to the concern about emerging Black Supremacy, and the effect that this may have on the country's future. In describing events and incidents, the reader may have to look between the lines for the implied attitudes and feelings that are inherent.

1. A Tribute to Darlas Mokone

Lessons learned #1

We met soon after I applied to join the EFF. Same day. I had just paid my registration fee of R10. Along with the application form, I attached a letter so that EFF would know right from the start that I am not a Marxist. I am a Christian, so I believe in God, shamelessly. Marxists are atheists so that is not my thing.

I had tried to join COPE in 2008. I attended the Congress of the People in Sandton. There was a sprinkling of white people at that event. But thereafter I had been treated like a spy. I could understand why when I later saw the party infighting. But it did not go well with COPE and me.

So when Agang set up shop, I tried to join that – online. For whatever reasons, that went nowhere.

Then EFF was launched in 2013 and seemed to resonate with the aspirations of youth. I liked that, so I decided to lend a hand. The same day that I handed in my application, with my proviso-letter and R10, I got a phone call. From Darlas. "Welcome to the movement". No conditions. And thereafter I was made to feel welcome. All the way to Atteridgeville, to the last EFF rally of the 2014 elections. Thirty thousand fighters, most of them in red, and only four white people. Two of whom were reporters from Europe! But everyone made me feel welcome. Safe and sound.

The EFF made an impressive start in the 2014 elections and did even better in the 2016 municipal elections. In Mpumalanga, it scored well above the national average. Darlas was appointed to be an EFF Councilor in Bushbuckridge. He did us proud.

He once said to me that living in deep rural Bushbuckridge, he had never been well acquainted with a white person before. We got on really well, and that seemed to intrigue him. But he warmed up and until last night when I visited him in hospital only hours before he died, we had a warm and genuine friendship. Sadly, he did not live to see EFF's parliamentary caucus increase from 25 seats to 44 seats. Or to see it assume the role of the official opposition party in three out of nine provinces – including in Mpumalanga which Darlas called home. But he could see it coming!

On the whole, I have found race relations in South Africa to be frigid. Compared to other periods that I have spent in Congo, Angola and Mozambique, I sense that relations here are strained. I also spent six years in Harare, Zimbabwe, where there was significant racial tension. But South Africa is not getting past it.

I recently read a book called <u>The Myth of Equality</u> – *uncovering the roots of injustice and privilege*. I know that I have enjoyed privilege all my life, and that Darlas had not. But my friendship with him assured me that this does not need to come between people. The author of that book is a pastor named Ken Wytsma. He wrote about one encounter that really got to me:

"I recently sat in Tel Aviv and listened to a discussion on peace and reconciliation by a Jewish women and a Palestinian man. What made this talk different from other peacemaking conversations I had witnessed was that both had lost a child in the violence between Arabs and Jews…

"As the story unfolded, I wanted to leave the room. I had begun to cry and, as a father, couldn't take any more. I was in the chair directly next to the man, though, so I felt obligated to stay where I was. I'm glad I did,

as the encounter of these two individuals turned out to be a life-changing moment for me.

"This man, this woman, and hundreds of others have banded together into a "parents' circle". They have all chosen the path of peace rather than revenge. Each has determined to end the cycle of violence by forgiving, pitying, understanding, humanizing, and empathizing with the story of the other.

"The Jewish mother said it well: 'The beginning of the end of violence comes when we see the humanity in the other. The beginning of violence comes when we forget the humanity in the other'...

"After a while, I began to think of my life against the backdrop of their story. I began to think about my family, my friends, and my community in relation to this story of reconciliation and redemption.

"What divides us?

This question – what divides us? – is mission-critical if we really want to build a Rainbow Nation.

The nation is divided into racial groups – black is the biggest, then coloured, then white, and lastly Indian.

The nation is divided by gender to the point that some call "femicide".

The nation is divided by age with only 5% of senior politicians under the age of 35, when half of the Electorate is under that age. This is not representative. Especially when you consider that only 5.4 percent of the population is 65 years of age, or older.

The ruling congress is divided into two factions. One is trying to clean house, while the other seems to be lost in denialism that it ever did anything wrong.

The loyal opposition is divided into liberal democrats and social democrats. The old guard is stepping on the brakes while the younger cadres are stepping on the accelerator of change.

Can't we just start a circle or a bridge of people - like Darlas and I - where Marxists can tolerate Christians? Where blacks can make whites feel at ease? Where whites can admit that privilege is part of the problem, not just poverty? Where Muslims and Christians can pray together? Where we can commit to looking for the humanity in the other, and to keep reminding ourselves that to forget that, is what feeds the cycle of alienation and violence?

The future of South Africa may not be in party platforms or political correctness at all. It may have more to do with friendship and solidarity across the racial divide, the gender divide, the religious divides, the age divide and the attitudes that have hardened on all sides.

Instead of "radical economic transformation" (RET) maybe we need to start with "radical attitudinal transformation" (RAT)?

Darlas and I learned not just to work together and dream together but to even like one another.

His family has lost a father, partner, brother, son and grandson. The EFF has lost a Councilor. C4L has lost a Board member. I have lost a dear friend. Rest in peace, Darlas Mokone.

1. Back-sliding from Rainbow campus to Zebra campus

Lessons learned #2

Everyone who reads or watches the News in South Africa knows about the Zondo Commission into State Capture. It is unraveling the issues raised in the <u>State of Capture</u> report written by former Public Protector Thuli Madonsela before her term of office ended. The big buzzword is *impunity*. People are "getting away with murder", so to speak. And there are other commissions to, and parliamentary oversight committees.

There has apparently not been a political will to do anything about it. So after years of on-again, off-again prosecution, ex-President Zuma comes forward with a new strategy – asking for a permanent stay of execution, on the grounds that he cannot possibly now get a fair trial. Because he has already been tried – in the court of public opinion.

The delays in cases reaching "the Bench" are legendary. To the extent that a good defense is never based on Content issues, but on Process. If you have a weak defense, just keep playing for time.

But aside from the high-profile "rich and famous", how does impunity play out at ground level? And to what extent is it just a strategy of clever lawyers? Or to what extent is the same Justice system being manipulated to protect some citizens and to target others?

That was the problem when Apartheid as a policy became *grand apartheid*, actually embedded in the law of the land. To what extent is impunity and black privilege actually systemic – particularly in the courts? In business, affirmative action is a version of black privilege. It gives the competitive edge to those who were "historically disadvantaged". One can understand this logic.

But when it comes to law enforcement - at the local level - how does this sense that Lady Justice has lost her blindfold play out? I have not been locked up for years – no, decades – on Robben Island, like the Treason Trialists. I have not organized an ambulance core, just to see my stretcher-bearers being killed because they are picking up soldiers from BOTH armies. But I have been unlawfully arrested; I have been burgled repeatedly for data (not hardware); I have received a letter from a government programme thanking me for a resignation that I never submitted; I have seen documentary evidence vaporize from the Hawks offices; and I have received numerous threats of death and deportation.

My personal experience – far from the televised testimonies of the rich and powerful (that contradict one another often enough to make you wonder "Which one is sowing the disinformation?") - is that not just media coverage (cif chapter 2) but the police, prosecutors and magistrates, are basically anti-white.

To some extent this might be a case of "implicit bias" which is unpacked in chapter 6. The majority of citizens are black, so one can predict the subjective way that they perceive reality. When objectively, the perception of the minority may be entirely different.

But it gets worse than that, into collusion of blacks against whites, and into the apparent "capture" of police and prosecutors by a local "casa nostra". That is Italian for "our house". It is otherwise known as the Mafia. Organized crime closes ranks with state structures, perhaps due to implicit bias. On top of the racial bias, there is a strong gender bias as well, stemming from affirmative action in favour of women. In a context of femicide at the national level, one can understand why these biases exist. I do understand and despise the history of apartheid and colonialism, and the way that women have been and are being treated.

But Lady Justice is still supposed to be wearing a blindfold. So it becomes problematic when she can be seen to be peaking.

Especially when an older, white, male foreigner takes on a younger black, female national in a court – it gets complicated! It basically creates judicial gridlock.

My testimony is not as dramatic as those televised accounts by the likes of Angelo Agrizzi (one of the bad guys) or Robert McBride (one of the good guys). But it is the *everyday* nature of my narrative that should be disturbing. Because it is happening all over the place and at every level. And my contention is that this is what Black Supremacy feels like to Everyman.

A Rainbow Campus

We bought our campus in 2001. By "we" I mean a group of about 12 families, both black and white. So there were about 25 shareholders in all. Because most of these investors were couples - who chose to each hold half of their family's shares. At the back of campus there were four rental homes, each already occupied by a white tenant family. We left these tenants in place to become our "cash cow". Meanwhile we occupied the farm house at the front of the campus, as our training centre.

We almost immediately started to sub-divide the campus, which was too big for our own purposes. Most of our training was for black youth. So we had black learners staying at the front campus for short courses and white tenants living at the back, about half a kilometer apart.

From time to time, a family of tenants would give notice and move out. Working through an estate agent, we would look for new tenants. After two years, I noticed that the estate agent only ever brought whites to view the houses, so I asked, why? "Oh, well, this is a white area" she told me. I protested. We live in a Rainbow Nation and anyone is welcome. But she was unable to bring any non-whites, possibly because she had no black clients?

So I spoke to our investors and they said they would be on the look-out for non-whites looking for a house to rent. I had been appointed one of two company directors. I spoke to my counterpart and told him that next time a house came up for rent, I would not rent it to another white family. This was becoming an issue with me. He disagreed. He said that company directors have a fiduciary duty to act in the best financial interest of their shareholders – so whoever came forward should be accepted immediately.

I mentioned affirmative action and I said that part of our remit was to establish a "Rainbow Campus". We must have a social bottom line as well as a financial one. Not just by hosting black learners at the front campus for short periods, with whites-only staying semi-permanently on the back campus. In fact, I had to leave to next available house vacant for 2 – 3 months until one of our investors found us a black tenant. A relative of theirs.

She was a fine tenant, a lawyer, who had been a magistrate and was promoted to HOD of Public Works in our province. She drove a nicer car than anyone else on campus! But she only wanted a one-year lease. She explained that her husband had died and left her a winfall, so she was busy building a family home in town. While it was being erected, she just needed a house for one year.

So this widow moved in with her children, and guess what? I kid you not! Within six months, every white family had left. The words "There goes the neighbourhood!" took on a whole new meaning.

After 10 months she came to me and asked me to release her from the 12-month lease, because her construction project was competed ahead of schedule. I complied, without claiming any penalties.

Restructuring

The sudden exodus of the tenants opened a new door. I approached the shareholders and asked if any of them were interested in converting the whole company share structure in such a way that there would only be four Class A shares, instead of the original configuration. Two shareholders expressed interest, so our auditors set up a very detailed Shareholder Agreement to guide this conversion. A third family offered to buy in, so that we could pay a "thank you" to the twenty-odd Class "B" shareholders now on their way out.

Now all four houses were occupied by blacks, one of whom was the new shareholder. The other three were tenants. I am reporting this because this owner-family became our "control experiment", so to speak. They have upgraded their house and they keep it in really good nick. They have been participative in company affairs and totally cooperative at all times.

What I learned from this is that tenants do not keep up their rental units well, leaving the landlord to watch helplessly while the property deteriorates. Only owners keep up their units. I have heard ex-DA Mayor Mashaba in Joburg complain about how tenants behave, until landlords just pull out. This leaves government holding the bag in terms of safety, fire, disputes, etc..

A Zebra Campus

It was over ten years before another white moved into one of these four homes, and it was yours truly. In the interim, the campus community had become entirely black. But a decade later, three of the four houses had deteriorated so badly, and the gardens were so overgrown, that I figured the only hope at reclaiming them was for me to be on campus full time - myself. As company director.

I cannot begin to describe the extent of the deterioration. It took me 6 months just to get the house that I occupied back to an acceptable living standard! For the first two weeks I caught at least one rat each night in my traps. De-rooting the bamboo which was rapidly overtaking the lawn could not be done manually – I had to hire a TLB! We unclogged drains and rebuilt kitchen cupboards and painted up a storm. That was five years ago now. That house has now been re-occupied by white tenants and is now looking very smart. They enjoy it.

But the drama was only just beginning. One of the remaining two tenants (now that I occupied one house and a black shareholder occupied another) was starting to skip rental payments. Whenever we approached him about missed payments, he got very stroppy. After 18 months of on-again-off-again rent, the landlord company passed a resolution to initiate eviction proceedings.

It took a very long time – almost a year, but we did get an Eviction Order. Even then he would not move out! He told the Magistrate that he was appealing his eviction in the High Court in Pretoria! He did start that process, but then he abandoned the case – and the house – about 6 months after the date of eviction. Yet he has never been charged with contempt of court.

Nor has he paid the Unpaid Rent, even though we did obtain a Warrant of Execution for what he owes the company (a Section 32 process). Almost three years have passed since the Judgment for his eviction and the Taxation of Costs has not been provided yet by the Magistrate's Court!

To make a long story short, I started the renovation on his house after he left, finally, and I later moved into it. You won't believe what I found when I re-possessed it:

- The Wendy house was full of his accumulated garbage. He never took it to out to the road
- So the rat infestation was almost as bad as the first house that I rescued
- The garden was overgrown like Tanglewood Forest
- There were broken windows everywhere
- The plumbing leaks were so bad that baseboards had rotted

from constantly wet floors
- Holes were kicked through doors and interior walls

The company's attorney has now started the Collections phase. But I kid you not - this man uses intimidation and demonization to fight back. Over a year after his departure, he was still driving onto the property and loading items (like a dog house) into his vehicle and driving off. I reported this to the police as Theft – they did nothing.

He still comes weekly in his bakkie to fetch several large drums of water from the fourth and last house which is still under dispute with the last black tenant. (Although neither of them contributes anything to our borehole pumping costs for that water.) When I screwed a cap onto the tap on the standpipe that he steals water from, he went and called out the police! A police escort for a thief!

Oh, did I mention that he has a job in the Premier's Office? Speaking of impunity...

A Tenant from Hell

The story of our company's fourth house could aptly be called "The Last Battle". This eviction process has been going on for over three years now and has generated more heat than light.

It started with the tenant – another widow – getting remarried and moving out, almost four years ago now. This was about the time that I myself moved onto the campus to launch Operation Revive. However, as her children were young adults and her new husband had his own place, she left her children on their own on campus. At least one was under 18 years of age. The older ones came and went periodically – they were at college. They strewed their garbage all over the place. Their Wendy house (a garden shed) literally collapsed into disrepair.

The bamboo invasion went wild, quite literally, and started to kill off indigenous trees. Death by choking. And to clog drains.

So we contacted our company attorney, who contacted her. He asked her to leave and we eventually met her with her attorney present, and came to an agreement that she would leave on an agreed date. Her attorney wrote down that agreement. But on the agreed date, she informed me that she has hired a new lawyer and she was going to "escalate". That was three years ago.

She has tried a new tack – installing third parties in the house, to plunder rental income from our company. Zimbabweans and Nigerians and relatives of the tenant who was evicted! Go figure. They have not been cooperative, in many ways that I will not bore you with. It can accurately be called a defiance campaign.

Meanwhile, I twice delivered letters of notice to the house, accompanied by our company's attorney – driving a vehicle with the law firm's insignia on it. I gathered together and bagged all the tenant garbage lying around and placed it on the car port of that house. (The municipality only picks up garbage one day a week, so that was my "staging area" until I loaded it and removed it to the road a few days later.)

For this she applied to the Family Court for a Protection Order against me. Not to deliver any more letters to the door of that house. Not to dump any more garbage there. And not to have any direct communication with her – only through her new lawyer.

When I sent her letters via her attorney, he replied that he was a lawyer, not an errand-runner, and that he would throw all my letters into the dust bin. That was the end of any meaningful communication with the tenant, because gender bias won the day and she was granted "protection" – from her landlord.

Then the allegations that I had violated the Protection Order started pouring in. One even before the date of the judgment when the Final Protection Order was issued! These were spurious but the third one led to my arrest. For the first time in my 66 years I spent a night in jail!

To his credit, the Magistrate saw through this ploy and released me the next day. The charges were later withdrawn by the State Prosecutor. Opening the way for me personally to sue both her and the Minister of Police for reputation loss. That case is moving along better than the "mother case" – because we actually want it to get to Trial as soon as possible. We are confident of winning. When someone is delaying their day in court, it is probable that they sense a risk of losing.

Meanwhile we had received two dates set for the Pre-Trial regarding the "mother case", and both fell through. On the first date, the court apologized that it had forgotten to inform the Tenant of the date. Nevertheless, we still had to pay our attorney for being prepared. The second time, her attorney called the day before the Pre-Trial and asked to punt it. There was then another long wait but it finally happened. Now a year has passed without a Trial date being set. Go figure!

So we then decided to approach the Mpumalanga Rental Housing Tribunal. This did not yet exist at the level of our province three years ago, so another process was set in motion. We have asked that both cases run concurrently – the "mother case" must be resolved by a court, but meanwhile the Tribunal can hear for us the matter of unpaid rent. For during landlord/tenant disputes, rental should continue to be paid. First the Tribunal offered mediation, but the tenant did not rock up. So they said they would subpoena her to a hearing before the full tribunal. Then we found out that the three-year contracts of all the Commissioners had expired. New names had been submitted to the Department of Human Settlements, but to date there have been no appointments.

Then along came the "lockdown" of the Covid-19 pandemic. Evictions and foreclosures are not the order of the day. To the landlord, it feels like tenants have all the rights. Does Ramaphosa realistically think that he can attract foreign investment into a context like this?

Interference

It is beyond belief that this is just all bungling or filibustering. Our company's legal fees are mounting, but it is double jeopardy because one of our company's income streams has dried up.

"Experience is a hard teacher – it gives the test first, and the lesson after." My testimony is that the Police protect the tenant; the Prosecutors target me; and the Magistrates make no effort to find a just and fair solution. It just drags on and on and on. Justice delayed is Justice denied.

Imagine the police arriving, very recently, with the evicted tenant – to guard him while he stole water. Again. He showed them that I had put a threaded cap onto the water tap on the stand pipe. I told the policemen that Finance Minister Tito Mboweni stated in his 2019 Budget speech that we must all accept the principle of *"the User must pay"*. This imposter got the tenant-from-hell on the phone. She told the police escort that she had authorized this gainfully employed official from the Premier's Office to fetch water there. Although she has never paid anything towards the borehole pumping costs, and does not reside on campus any longer.

The house has been abandoned, standing empty for almost a year. Because most of its windows were broken in a domestic dispute involving the "squatters" (Herman Mashaba's term) who were occupying it last year. They moved out that very day according to witnesses, as I was away overseas at the time. Essentially the house was rendered un-inhabitable. We got a quotation to fix the windows from a glass company that came out to measure it up. It will cost R3700.

The police protected this thief while he stole our water, then they left – taking the threaded cap with them. Even though I had just showed them the thief's Eviction Order and the Title Deed to the campus *in the company's name*. To my way of thinking, this is not just impunity... it is stealing, intimidation, and Black Supremacy. If this is the way that blacks want to run Azania, then I am increasingly inclined to empathize with whites, coloureds, Ba Baroa and blacks who want to follow the path of Partition and establish a distinct and non-racial Orania.

1. Gaslighting

<u>Lessons learned #3</u>

After the 2019 elections, I received this disturbing email from Durban:

"Thursday, 16 May 2019

Abahlali baseMjondolo press statement

Break-in at the Abahlali baseMjondolo Office

This morning we arrived at our office, which is in the Diakonia Centre in central Durban, to find that there had been a break in last night. The hard drives of two computers, an external hard drive and the keys to our safe were taken. The cash in the safe was not touched and other easily saleable items, like our microwave, television, cameras and mobile sound system were not taken.

It was clear that the thieves were looking for information, not money. One of the hard drives that they took is old and would have very little resale value. However, the two hard drives, and the external hard drive that were taken, do contain lots of information about our movement, including the audited database of our membership which is a spreadsheet with every members' name, age, phone number, ID or passport number and other details, details of all our branches, our correspondence with other progressive organisations in South Africa and elsewhere in the world, and so on.

It is clear that this break in was the work of intelligence. We can't be certain about the motivation for the break in but our immediate suspicion is that it is linked to our opposition to the gangster mayor of Durban, and all the gangster councillors that support her.

We are currently waiting for the police to finish at the crime scene. Once they have left we will be able to see if anything else was taken, such as files, documents etc.

We repeat our call for the immediate removal of Zandile Gumede from her position as mayor, and for the strongest possible protection for the witnesses who will testify against her.

We will not be intimidated. We have nothing to hide. The struggle continues.

Land & Dignity!"

This kind of break-in or "burglary" has repeatedly happened to me/us on our campus. Once they robbed our three clumsy desktops, leaving the keyboards and monitors behind. They also left 12 laptops in the training room that night! Even the police told us: "This was a data robbery".

Our public engagement has never been quite as strident as *Abahlali baseMjondolo*. But we have been outspoken and resilient, including sometimes on national media platforms. I am not boasting, I am privileged, and I know it. In this chapter, I will resist commenting again on Land Reform.

There is no doubt in my mind, reading the reports to Parliament about the spying on citizens by the State Security Agency – and its clandestine shadow the Principle Agent Network – that we are being watched. I operate on the assumption that my phones are wiretapped, that my emails are read by more people than the addressees, and that they know about my movements - and my personal life. Even the honourable Chief Justice Mokoeng Mokoeng became aware that he was under surveillance, and he gave some good advice – just ignore it and get on with your life... keeping legal and upright at all times.

Why do people want to invade the privacy of others and keep tabs on them?

The Movie

Gaslight is a Hollywood mystery-thriller film, made in 1944. It is adapted from Patrick Hamilton's 1938 play *Gas Light*, about a woman whose husband slowly manipulates her into believing that she is going insane.

The term has come into popular parlance as a synonym to "blame-shifting" – but on a grander scale. We all know about blame-games, but that could be just one incident. Whereas when someone is "gaslighting" you, they are going to scale with the blame-shifting.

According to Google: *"Gaslighting" is used to describe abusive behavior, specifically when an abuser manipulates information in such a way as to make a victim question his or her sanity. Gaslighting intentionally makes someone doubt their memories or perception of reality.*

So when the police arrest you, for example, and throw you into jail in full view of your neighbors and friends, this is both abusive and "gaslighting" if they have manipulated information in such a way that you begin to doubt yourself, and your own integrity. Maybe the police are right about you? After all, they wear uniforms!

Getting a court order to seize property, or a Protection Order (which comes with a ready-made arrest warrant attached to it, good for five years) does not just involve the police. The prosecutors and magistrates are also involved. A court order without a Magistrate's signature is invalid. This is where the term "systemic" comes to mind.

Crimes have to be both investigated and prosecuted. The SAPS does the investigating and the NPA does the prosecution. If there is not very good articulation between these two functions, law enforcement loses its lustre. This was why they closed the Scorpions, because it had tandem powers – to investigate and to prosecute. As a result, it had a great record at nailing people for corruption. Part of the intentionality of State Capture was to shut it down. By the time Hugh Glenister won his case at the Constitutional Court, it was too late. It was gone.

Another part of the intentionality was to "capture" the NPA. They say that a fish rots from the head and that is what happened to the NPA. Now it is rotten through and through, right down to the Magistrate's Court level. Sacking the former NDPP and replacing him with a new one was the first step on the road to recovery. But she was and is still surrounded by the rot.

Then the president approved the new NDPP's request to establish her own investigative unit - inside the NPA. What does that tell you about her confidence in the SAPS? I second the emotion. The head of this new investigative unit was selected only after the 2019 elections. Both these ladies deserve our daily prayers. The roll-out of Justice depends on it.

Spies gather intelligence about you to hurt you. They twist it, like when my own family was told - by a policeman - that I had been making porn videos! This kind of innuendo is blended by your adversaries with their own biases – until it reaches the grand scale of "gaslighting". Our evicted ex-tenant is a black official working in the Premier's office. For many years his boss was David Mabuza, not just one of those "vindictive triumphalists" but also a member of the Premier League. I am a white foreigner who has not been afraid to blow the whistle.

This official has abused his power more than once to tarnish my reputation. He intimidates. He does not pay his debts. To injure me.

But I took him on – I sued him for Defamation. I won, in the Regional Court – R50 000 plus costs. Again, we have a judgment and a warrant of execution, but will the Sheriff seize his assets? Think again! The Sheriff had previously tried that once – he nabbed this fellow's car. He held it for several months, threatening to auction it off. But the Premier's Office was all over him from the very day that he nabbed it. The system protects some and targets others.

Why does the magistrate sign an Eviction Order then not enforce it? What use is a Section 32 Warrant of Execution when the same court delays ad infinitum in producing a taxation of costs, and when the Sheriff is too intimidated to seize any assets? What is Black Supremacy, and what does it feel like to Everyman?

Discrediting, Demonization & Destabilization

We cannot be sure who exactly is mixed up in this cat-and-mouse game. By their very nature, spy games are conducted in an ethos of smoke-and-mirrors. But I have been warned by these cloak-and-dagger tenants that I myself am under investigation by "intelligence"; that the Premier's bodyguards will be coming to arrest me; that I am "a dead man walking"; that I will be sent back to Canada; and that they know about my health challenges. So be it.

We live in a country where blacks out-number whites ten-to-one. They speak languages, often in our very presence, purposely to exclude us and remind us that we are "foreign". (This is one reason that the "melting pot" approach of a lingua franca serves some other countries very well – it reduces exclusion.) Once they get "dirt" on you, it spreads like veld fire. Gossip, cell phones, social media, and "implicit bias" are all used to alienate you. Even revenge porn may be deployed by these bent citizens who delight in hurting foreigners.

We have seen what xenophobia can do, when Mob Psychology kicks in. (The IQ of a mob is the lowest IQ of anyone in the mob.)

They are using deprivation tactics by not paying the rent, or else the levies, to keep the company's cash-flow positive. Then they run up your legal bills by getting the courts to keep churning out allegations, applications for Protection Orders (I am now on my fourth case in as many years, all of them nonsense), and interminable delays. They use the Stalingrad defense strategy, punting court dates time and again. Public structures protect some people and target others. They may respond that they exist to protect the good guys and to target the bad guys. Fair enough, but why does that always correspond to our racial fault lines? Are they not just playing the race card?

I have repeatedly attempted to report crimes at the local SAPS precinct. On the following four occasions, I was turned away and told that there was already a case open. I was rejected when:

1. My vehicle was tampered with. Muti was poured into the radiator. I ended up having to replace the bakkie's engine. This was only two days after a death threat. *Attempted murder?*
2. I was thinning out a thicket of running bamboo on our

campus to save an indigenous Albizia tree from choking. They came with a chain saw and cut down the Albizia tree, out of spite. *Malicious damage?*

3. They steal assets from the campus with impunity. In one case, there is an eye-witness, but the police do nothing. *Theft?*

4. Once I spoke to a Nigerian "squatter" about keeping the front gate closed. He had just opened it, driven through it and proceeded without closing it. This is unlawful on a farm. (We grow tree spinach and our neighbours pasture cows, goats and sheep.) He quickly parked his car and came after me. As I slipped in the front door, he kicked it open, breaking the lock. I was able to move a desk behind the door to keep him out. *Assault?*

Our company staff are traumatized. They have been directly intimidated and they fear that for carrying out my directives on campus, violence will be visited on them – at home in their township. One staff member approached the same Family Court, with one of our attorneys, to apply for a Protection Order, because of his genuine fears in this regard. He was told to leave, even though one of our company attorneys accompanied him. The courts protect some people and target others.

The charges that they have trumped up take a Civil dispute to a new level – Criminal charges. A violation of a Protection Order can earn you a criminal record for the rest of your life. No doubt in my case, they want to leverage my deportation from that?

Tenant collusion

There are obvious instances of collusion. I have mentioned the one where the fellow coming to steal our water called in the police and had them call the tenants who have not yet been evicted, to have them authorize him to steal our water. What is conspiracy? What is organized crime? Were these tenants that the police called on the phone not aiding and abetting a robbery?

I called on a guard to bear witness in a court-hearing about a Protection Order application. Court had not opened yet when the Magistrate called us into her chambers. While we discussed "points of order" related to the case in there, the other tenant came into the court room and threatened our witness' life. When we complained to the court, upon learning of this, the magistrate told us to get a lawyer to report it. The lawyer shared a proverb with me: "An eagle does not chase a fly."

In early 2019, we had another burglary. He got away with two laptops, but not before I shot him at point-blank range. Then he took off in a big hurry into the darkness! He (or they) have been back again around Easter 2019. This time between our burglar alarm and my handgun, they did not succeed in robbing any hardware. Or data.

They rarely catch a burglar, so you actually never know who is the burglar, who is the squatter, or who is the tenant. But it would not surprise me to find "all of the above" having a drink together at a shabeen the over week-end. It is becoming a blur.

I am beginning to think that Partition makes some sense. If two cultures cannot abide in the same space together without conflict, why not separate them? The litmus test is whether different religions or ethnic groups are "frequently antagonistic" to one another. If so, they have a right to self-determination.

Yet when I watch the Zondo Commission or read the newspaper, I wonder if there isn't some connection to my experiences of so-called law enforcement, and the reason that, in the whole State Capture saga, there have been so few arrests and even fewer convictions. Has anyone been sentenced so far? Now some voices are saying that they should be offered amnesty.

How can analysts see through the new Public Protector's whitewash of the Estima Dairy project, and not notice the reality of my experience at the local level? The ex-President asks for a permanent stay of execution for his corruption case. That was turned down, so now he wants to appeal to the Constitutional Court. Will the court say to the company that because it has not succeeded in evicting her in real time, she should stay permanently? It's arguing in a circle.

The system protects some, and targets others. And it is getting systemic, it is not just ad hoc. Black Privilege is a reality, and it arises from something deeper – a deep attitude of Black Supremacy. From spying to policing to prosecuting, the system that I have experienced is anti-white and anti-foreigner. I remain in South Africa for its great weather, not for its socialization.

1. PEACE BUILDING: From Parties to Coalitions

Forty-eight parties contested the 2019 elections in South Africa, and only fourteen of them won at least one seat in the National Assembly. So thirty-four did not succeed.

It costs R200 000 just to register as a part, so almost R7 million Rand was spent that could perhaps have been spent in other ways?

I like what the Rev Jesse Jackson once said: *"Leadership has a harder job to do than just choose sides. It must bring sides together."*

South African Democracy uses the "PR system", that is proportional representation. This model of Democracy suits the proliferation of parties better than the other model, where each constituency votes for a member of parliament. In that model, there tends to be a contest between two large parties, or perhaps three. So as we watch the ANC's majority get smaller and smaller, we are not seeing a second large party emerge as an alternative. Rather, we are seeing a flotilla of smaller parties emerge.

We have to work on this. Too many small parties just splinters the opposition vote. Voters get confused or worse yet, indignant at the waste of resources and the implied self-promotion of people starting their own parties. So they withdraw their consent from democracy and the voter turn-out sinks. In the last election in 2019, less than half of the eligible Electorate voted.

Baby and Bathwater

As a youth worker, I was appalled at the way that Julius Malema and his team were treated by the ANC when he was head of its Youth League. Here are a few clips from pieces that I wrote for the media at that time. I was trying to warn the ANC that its so-called disciplinary action could lead to another split. (COPE had already "divorced" the ANC by this time, and had gone on to win 30 seats in parliament.)

The story of Joseph is about one of the great successes in African leadership. But Joseph was disliked and derided by his own older brothers. One day he came to visit them at their place of work. They saw him coming and said to one another, "Here comes the dreamer". They hated his ambitions - which could sideline them. In their minds, youth should be subservient and not challenge the older brothers. They plotted his destruction.

Is the ANC doing the same to Julius Malema? Or is he the one bringing the ANC into disrepute? The older brothers first disliked him because he voiced once too often some crazy ideas that allegedly scared away foreign investors. They have to run the country's economy now, like the sons of Israel had to run the old man Jacob's affairs. They got threatened by Malema and you could hear them saying cynically, "Here comes the

dreamer... he should fall into line, and stop talking about regime change".
Now the stakes are higher and closer to home – change of leadership.

God has his own plans. Joseph sank pretty low, even into slavery and prison. But then his fortunes changed and one day he was appointed ruler in Egypt by the head of state, the Pharoah. He set up a food bank that ironically, in the end, saved his own brothers. One can only wonder where Malema will be in a couple of decades time, even if the ANC succeeds in sidelining him this year?

Malema not only speaks on behalf of youth, he speaks in the way they speak. They have been getting a bad deal, and they are waking up to it. More than half the youth of today have been born since the dawn of Democracy in 1995. During that period the number of jobs has shrunk by 3 million and the population increased by 10 million (all under 17 today). Meanwhile, the average COSATU worker stays in the same job for 43 years. Go figure! There are few opportunities at entry level for school leavers, caused by the grid lock of the older brothers holding down all the jobs left in the work place. No wonder the youth dream dreams! As leader of the Youth League, Malema has to vocalize the plight of Generation J. He doesn't just speak for them, he is one of them and his brand of defiance is like them.

Can the ANC throw out the baby without the bathwater?

David was another younger brother. He was left behind to tend the herds while the older brothers went off to war. But they could not sort out that Philistine champion called Goliath. Every day he came up to the front line and hurled insults – at God! They couldn't stop him.

Until David came up to bring some fresh supplies from the farm. He couldn't believe it! His proven courage and determination kicked in and he offered to fight the giant. His older brothers scoffed at him. "You are just a boy," they told him. This sounds like the ANC speaking to Juju. If his ideas succeeded, who would be bringing who into disrepute!?

The lines of disparity in South Africa today are as graphic as that line between the Philistine army and the Israelites. It's only ten kilometers from Thembisa to Irene - from people living in survival mode to others living in surplus mode. The giant that shouts insults at God every day in South Africa is Poverty, not Goliath. It is offensive. And 74 per cent of the unemployed in South Africa are youth. It's a time bomb.

King Saul offered David his armour for the encounter. David tried it on and rejected it. He took his own technology and won the day. Good for King Saul for letting him do it his way! Einstein said that you won't solve a crisis by applying the same kind of thinking that caused it in the first place. That's what the ANC are trying to do. The same old boys who failed to solve the problem of unemployment in the first place are hanging on to a failed approach. David rejected Saul's armour – and won the day. The ANC needs to back off and give the Youth League some room to manoevre. A new kind of thinking is surely needed, and Malema has every right (even a responsibility) to voice the discontent of youth. For no one will be affected more that they will be by decisions made in 2012. It is time to listen to youth like King Saul did. This may not exonerate Malema for his indiscretions, but what message is suspended him sending to Generation J? They are already suspended, in limbo between leaving school and finding work - which is precisely why he has been making so much noise!

Twenty years after Joseph was sold out by his older brothers, they came to him without realizing it. That young dreamer had changed so much, and being dressed in local attire, his own brothers didn't recognize him. So he tested them severely, only to find that over the decades of separation, they too had deeply changed. Now they were protective of their youngest brother – Benjamin - not cruel to him. When he was convinced of this fundamental change of behaviour, he couldn't hold it back any longer and disclosed his identity to them.

The ANC needs this kind of deep reconciliation – generational not racial. The old boys club cannot afford to lose the bathwater with the baby! Youth needs to be at the forefront – not sidelined.

Party-building mode

So when the EFF was formed, I decided to make a few contributions. These were mostly at the local level, and led on to my cherished friendship with Darlas Mokone highlighted in chapter 25. I was delighted to see the EFF rise to the status of official opposition in my home province of Mpumalanga after the 2019 elections. And heart-broken that Darlas didn't live to see it.

My major contribution to the 2014 election was to record and post a video on YouTube of a good old Canadian folk tale called Mouseland. I did not write it. It was written a long, long time ago by Clarence Gillis, a trade unionist and politician from Nova Scotia. It was later popularized by Tommy Douglas, one of the most influential Canadians ever. I see many parallels between Tommy Douglas and Julius Malema.

I just tweaked it a bit, to fit South Africa, and then posted in on YouTube. Animal Farm is a (much longer) send-up of Communism. Mouseland is a send-up of Capitalism. Here is the revised text:

Mouseland

This is a story about a place called Mouseland... because the EFF also has a good story to tell!

Mouseland was a place where all the little mice lived and played, were born and died. And they lived much the same as you and I do, riding in taxis and watching football.

They even had a Parliament. And every five years they had an election. They used to walk to the polls and cast their ballots. Some of them even got a ride to the polls. (And got a ride for the next five years afterwards too!) They were just like you and me. And every time on election day all the little mice used to go to the ballot box and they used to elect a government. A government made up of big, fat, white cats.

Now if you think it strange that mice should elect a government made up of cats, you just look at the history of South Africa and maybe you'll see that they aren't the only ones who get confused about who to elect!

Now I'm not saying anything against the cats. They were nice fellows. They conducted their government with dignity. They passed good laws - that is, laws that were good for cats. But the laws that were good for cats weren't very good for mice. One of the laws said that mouseholes had to be big enough so a cat could get his paw in. Another law said that mice could only travel at certain speeds - so that a cat could get his breakfast without too much effort.

All the laws were good laws. For cats. But, oh, they were hard on the mice. And life was getting harder and harder. And when the mice couldn't put up with it any more, they decided something had to be done about it. So they went en masse to the polls. They voted the white cats out. They voted in the black cats.

Now the black fat cats had put up a terrific campaign. They said: "All that Mouseland needs is more vision." They said: "The trouble with Mouseland is those round mouseholes we all use. If you vote us in we envision square mouseholes." And they did it! And the square mouseholes were twice as big as the round mouseholes, and now the cat could get both his paws in. And life was tougher than ever.

And when the mice just couldn't take that anymore, they tried a government of half black cats and half white cats. And they called that a ruling alliance.

You see, my friends, the trouble wasn't with the colour of the cat. The trouble was - that they were cats. And because they were cats, they naturally looked after cats instead of mice.

Presently there came along one little mouse who had an idea. My friends, watch out for that plump little fellow with an idea! And he said to the other mice, "Look fellows, why do we keep on electing a government made up of cats? Why don't we elect a government made up of mice?" "Oooooh," they said, "he's a Communist. He hasn't paid his taxes - lock him up!" So they put him in jail. On an island... in the sea.

But I want to remind you: that you can lock up a mouse and you can lock up a man - but you can't lock up an idea.

Coalition-building mode

In the run-up to the 2019 elections, I became very worried about the tone and content of Malema's rhetoric, and I told him so. My worry was that if the ANC dropped below the 50 percent threshold and a window of opportunity opened for the opposition parties to form a coalition government (some polls anticipated this), that the smaller parties would find it hard to coalesce.

This is still my worry, and one of the reasons is this rising tide of Black Supremacy.

Going forward, we need to build fewer, stronger parties and to focus our efforts and resources on Coalition-building. But this cannot happen if these parties are "frequently antagonistic" to one another. That will only take us down the road to Partition – a Two-State Solution.

The alternative emerging to ANC government is not another party – it is a coalition of parties. You don't have to be a rocket-scientist to figure that out. The trending is that both big parties are shrinking and the smaller parties are growing robustly. The growth points in the 2019 elections were the EFF on the Left and the Freedom Front Plus on the Right. Call it polarization if you will.

But the writing is on the wall – for both the ANC and for the opposition parties: "*You have been weighed in the balance and found wanting*". We voted out white supremacy – the white cats. We need to vote out the fat black cats next. And vote in the mice.

The then-Chairman of EFF put it this way: "*Coalitions are not necessarily about policy convergence. In fact, it's the opposite because there's no need to have coalitions with people that you agree with.*"

This was echoed by then-DA leader Maimane: "*There must be shared principles and agenda that all parties agree to when they enter a coalition.*"

This will involve some new tools – to arrive at "tolerable compromises" as a coalition of parties that have "boggeral" in common. Mechanisms like rank-choice voting and indicative voting can help a Coalition to function smoothly.

In fact, the cornerstone of the Coalition will be to clean up government and to empower the National Assembly. For this kind of Coalition is the best way to outgrow the ANC's bent to "vanguardism". Its party structure the NEC should not be running our country. The State should be run by its National Assembly. That is the way that the Constitution reads.

The spirit of Coalition governments is implicit in these famous words of Nelson Mandela, which I am quoting for the third time. Repetition is a way of emphasizing, and I believe that if parties and party leaders could adopt these words as "shared principles" (to quote Maimane), then Coalition-building could lead on – to peace building:

> **"During my lifetime I have dedicated myself to this struggle of the African people. I have fought against white domination, and I have fought against black domination. I have cherished the ideal of a democratic and free society in which all persons will live together in harmony and with equal opportunities. It is an ideal which I hope to live for. But, my lord, if needs be, it is an ideal for which I am prepared to die."**

Post-Disaster Recovery

When the Covid-19 pandemic appeared, there were different strategies to choose from. Some countries like Sweden chose to minimize government intervention. Other nations in the EU and the USA adopted "mitigation" strategies. Because the pathogen arrived relatively late in South Africa, government went for "suppression", intervening early and hard – and wisely so.

By the same token, there are more than one "offramps" or exit strategies. Some countries will remain under lockdown longer, and some will try to de-escalate the confinement sooner, perhaps gradually. Because there was an economic earthquake as well as a medical emergency.

The short-term future will be the period from the point that we reach "herd immunity" until a vaccine is found. The long-term future will only come after a vaccine is rolled out. From the offramp that we take out of confinement, to the day that we can be vaccinated and feel totally safe again, we will be living in something of a twilight zone.

Disasters happen when a natural calamity (a storm, a plague, etc.) smashes into *vulnerability*. This book is about our vulnerability, and I don't mean the number of hospital beds or worse yet ventilators. Deeper than that, it is about the way that we get along - *or don't get along* - as we co-habitate this southern tip of Africa. This reality weakens the social cohesion that we need going forward. Diversity should be a resource that makes us proud.

An old proverb says: "All hands on deck when the ship's on fire". The good ship Rainbow is burning. A veld fire is passing through that will burn out a lot of underbrush – to allow for new growth when it gets green again. The trees and animals that can resist can emerge stronger. God grant us the resilience to learn from the challenges we face. And the courage to join forces and not let the pandemic break us apart. Ironically, this pathogen does not discriminate. Black or white, rich or poor, male or female, educated or not – it goes after everyone. The elderly are at risk more than children. May a new growth arise that will regard Diversity as our strength.

---

[1] https://www.elections.org.za/NPEDashboard/app/dashboard.html#[1]

---

1. https://www.elections.org.za/NPEDashboard/app/dashboard.html

Did you love *Orania and Azania*? Then you should read *Rich Man, Poor Woman, Bogyman, Thief*[2] by CO Stephens and William O'Dowda!

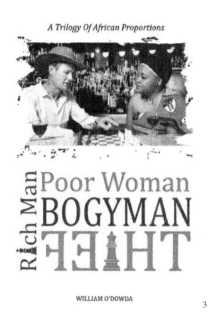

A Trilogy Of African Proportions

Rich Man Poor Woman BOGYMAN THIEF

WILLIAM O'DOWDA

3

The title has a familiar poetic ring to it. It is the second half of a rhyme that goes back to 1475, when William Caxton wrote a book about games *The Game and Playe of the Cheese*. It was a divination game, about who you were going to marry. Then AA Milne recycled it in 1927, in *Now We Are Six*. It is a playful turn of phrase, but serious too. So it is both traditional and relevant, like the book, which has recycled "beggar man" as "bogyman", to fit the narrative. And for gender balance, "poor man" has changed to "poor woman"... in keeping with the times.

Book 1 is the baseline narrative – a true story about someone who wasn't true. One reviewer of this book Black Queen White King Check

---

2. https://books2read.com/u/b5ZaOR

3. https://books2read.com/u/b5ZaOR

Mate wrote: "It is a cautionary tale, and it would be maudlin and tacky if it were not so interesting and well written." It exposes core themes of ancient versus modern, human rights versus the rights of the collective, and civil versus criminal.

Book 2 continues the narrative and then gets deep into issues related to customary marriage. This is very relevant in Africa, where most marriages by far adhere to these ancient customs. Which were shared by patriarchs like Isaac and Rebecca, Ruth and Boaz, right up to the late great rapper HHP and his "ex". All the way to the Supreme Court of Appeal in 2020 - disputing whether their customary marriage was valid or not. His family says that all the rites were not completed. Whereas she claims that because they lived together for three years, she has a right to his estate. Do gender rights trump aboriginal rights?

White King is Dead, Long Live Black Queen also revisits three historic inter-racial marriages, from Krotoa of the Sandlopers to Trever Noah's parents. Quoting the book reviewer again: "This is a fascinating look at South Africa through the eyes of a foreigner who has really made an effort to learn more than the average South Africa (black or white) knows about things.

Book 3 get positively controversial (pun intended). Friendly Fire in the Cathedral uses the issue of "HIV endangerment" as a litmus test, to discern whether the bride was ever sincere. If she wasn't, she was similar to the two South African's who tested positive early in the coronavirus crisis, who then "jumped quarantine" in KwaZulu-Natal. They were tracked down by contact-tracing, arrested, and charged with attempted murder. This books re-visits pestilences past, from the Black Plague right up to Covid-19, and applies lessons learned to the baseline narrative.

The author concludes that HIV endangerment may be over-criminalized in some settings, such as the HIV and AIDS pandemic in North America. In that context, it was viewed mainly as a sexually transmitted disease, mainly in the Gay community, and thus acquired double-jeopardy in terms of stigmatization. Whereas in

Africa is was much like Covid-19, knowing no boundaries of male, female, rich, poor, black, white, national or foreigner. In this context, HIV endangerment is a crime. But it is one that has been rarely prosecuted, because gender rights seem to trump victim rights. Even when it may have been weaponized to snafu the groom's estate.

The trilogy is autobiographical, written under a nome de plume to keep it as generic and informative as possible.

Also by CO Stephens

Opa Waxes Prophetic
Orania and Azania
Rich Man, Poor Woman, Bogyman, Thief

About the Publisher

Mbokodo Publishers is your choice service provider and partner in the publishing business. We make your business our business in order to understand your needs, tastes and challenges better so we could provide you with the most efficient services imaginable.

Our professional and committed staff and personnel are always ready to assist you whenever you contact us. So drop us an email or simply call or visit our offices and this could be the beginning of a positive change in your life!

We look forward to being of ultimate assistance to you our dear prospective clients. For more information with regards to our offered products and services, please email us, mbokodopublishers@gmail.com

We look forward to hearing from you soon. God bless you!

Regards,

Publisher

Printed by BoD™in Norderstedt, Germany